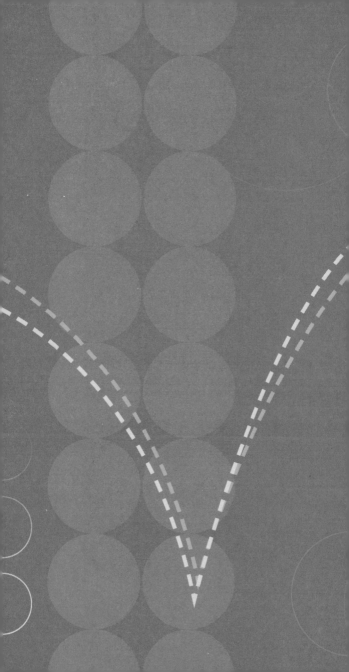

To:

....

Run in such a way
as to get the prize ...
a crown that will last forever.

1 Corinthians 9:24-25

From:

....

Slam Dunk! God's Words of Life
from the NIV Sports Devotional Bible
Copyright © 2004 by The Zondervan Corporation
ISBN 0-310-80600-3

The devotionals in this gift book were taken from the
Sports Devotional Bible, New International Version,
Dave Branon, General Editor.

Requests for information should be addressed to:
Inspirio, the gift group of Zondervan
Grand Rapids, Michigan 49530
http://www.inspiriogifts.com

Associate Publisher: Tom Dean
Compiler: Robin Schmitt
Design Manager: Val Buick
Designer: Amy Peterman

Printed in China
04 05 06/ HK/ 5 4 3 2 1

SLAM DUNK!

**God's Words of Life from
the NIV Sports Devotional Bible**

God's Word of Life on

ADVICE

Listen, my son, to your father's instruction
and do not forsake your mother's teaching.
They will be a garland to grace your head.
And a chain to adorn your neck.

Proverbs 1:8-9

Plans fail for lack of counsel,
but with many advisers they succeed.

Proverbs 15:22

Let the wise listen and add to their learning,
and let the discerning get guidance.

Proverbs 1:5

Listen to advice and accept instruction,
and in the end you will be wise.

Proverbs 19:20

Many advisers make victory sure.

Proverbs 11:14

ADVICE

The pleasantness of one's friend
  springs from his earnest counsel.

Proverbs 27:9

Wisdom is found in those who take advice.

Proverbs 13:10

Blessed is the man
  who does not walk in the counsel of the wicked
or stand in the way of sinners
  or sit in the seat of mockers.
But his delight is in the law of the LORD,
  and on his law he meditates day and night.

Psalm 1:1-2

First seek the counsel of the LORD.

1 Kings 22:5

Trust in the LORD with all your heart
  and lean not on your own understanding;
in all your ways acknowledge him,
  and he will make your paths straight.

Proverbs 3:5-6

ADVICE

Make plans by seeking advice.

Proverbs 20:18

*If any of you lacks wisdom, he should ask God,
who gives generously to all without finding fault,
and it will be given to him.*

James 1:5

He will be called
Wonderful Counselor, Mighty God.

Isaiah 9:6

*Jesus said, "When he, the Spirit of truth, comes, he
will guide you into all truth."*

John 16:13

A wise man listens to advice.

Proverbs 12:15

I am always with you, LORD;
you hold me by my right hand.
You guide me with your counsel,
and afterward you will take me into glory.

Psalm 73:23-24

These tall kids who are pretty good basketball players are listening to too many people who tell them how good they are and not enough to people who tell them that they are not quite ready for the NBA.

Sometimes these kids make themselves eligible for the draft—thus giving up their amateur status—and then fail to get drafted.

Those kids got really bad advice.

So did Rehoboam (2 Chronicles 10).

Rehoboam did do something right: He asked for two opinions, not just for one. His problem: How was he going to answer the people who had requested that he lighten their workload? He took that problem to two different groups of people.

The older people said, "Lighten up on the folks and they'll be your subjects." The younger people replied, "Hey, pour it on. Let them know who's boss."

Whose advice would you take? Rehoboam needed to exercise wisdom and good leadership when making his decision. He listened to the younger advisors. As a result, he burdened the people with work, and they rebelled.

The wisdom of accepting good advice is something God expects of all of us. It is part of the responsibility we have as God's people to seek and trust those who are willing to share their wisdom with us. To whom are you listening?

ANGER

Wise men turn away anger.

Proverbs 29:8

Everyone should be quick to listen, slow to speak and slow to become angry, for man's anger does not bring about the righteous life that God desires.

James 1:19-20

A patient man has great understanding,
    but a quick-tempered man displays folly.

Proverbs 14:29

In your anger do not sin. Do not let the sun go down while you are still angry.

Ephesians 4:26

An angry man stirs up dissension,
    and a hot-tempered one commits many sins.

Proverbs 29:22

Refrain from anger and turn from wrath;
    do not fret—it leads only to evil.

Psalm 37:8

ANGER

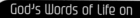

A fool gives full vent to his anger,
but a wise man keeps himself under control.

Proverbs 29:11

*As God's chosen people, holy and dearly loved,
clothe yourselves with compassion, kindness,
humility, gentleness and patience. Bear with each
other and forgive whatever grievances you may
have against one another. Forgive as the Lord forgave you. And over all these virtues put on love,
which binds them all together in perfect unity.*

Colossians 3:12-14

*If it is possible, as far as it depends on you, live at
peace with everyone.*

Romans 12:18

ANGER

As churning the milk produces butter …
so stirring up anger produces strife.

Proverbs 30:33

*Get rid of all bitterness, rage and anger, brawling
and slander, along with every form of malice.*

Ephesians 4:31

Jesus said, "Blessed are the peacemakers
for they will be called sons of God."

Matthew 5:9

Better a patient man than a warrior,
a man who controls his temper than one who
takes a city.

Proverbs 16:32

*Love is patient, love is kind. It does not envy, it
does not boast, it is not proud. It is not rude, it is
not self-seeking, it is not easily angered, it keeps
no record of wrongs.*

1 Corinthians 13:4-5

ANGER

John Wooden and Bob Knight have a lot of things in common. Both were well-known college men's basketball coaches. They were both great strategists. They could motivate their players to do tremendous things on the basketball court. These men got the most out of their players, and they won several championships.

If Wooden and Knight are so much alike, then why is there such a difference of opinion about these two men? Why is John Wooden held in such high regard while Bob Knight is viewed with less respect?

Part of the answer lies in Proverbs 15:1. John Wooden discovered a way to get his point across to his players, officials and other teams—both in practice and at games—using the "gentle answer" method. Bob Knight, on the other hand, employed the "harsh word" method. One turned away wrath; the other stirred up anger.

If we want to honor God with our words and actions, we'll strive to turn away anger with words that are kind and with actions that are thoughtful.

Our reputation is at stake when we respond to people. But more important, our character before God is being formed through our conversations and deeds. We can make a choice of how to respond to people that will affect how we are viewed and how we please God.

ASSISTING OTHERS

Seek justice,
  encourage the oppressed.
Defend the cause of the fatherless,
  plead the case of the widow.

Isaiah 1:17

Jesus said, "Come, you who are blessed by my Father; take your inheritance, the kingdom pre- pared for you since the creation of the world. For I was hungry and you gave me something to eat, I was thirsty and you gave me something to drink, I was a stranger and you invited me in, I needed clothes and you clothed me, I was sick and you looked after me, I was in prison and you came to visit me."

Matthew 25:34-36

Give to everyone who asks you.

Luke 6:30

Do not forget to do good and to share with others, for with such sacrifices God is pleased.

Hebrews 13:16

We must help the weak, remembering the words the Lord Jesus himself said: "It is more blessed to give than to receive."

Acts 20:35

ASSISTING OTHERS

Share your food with the hungry
    and ... provide the poor wanderer with shelter—
when you see the naked, ... clothe him,
    and [do not] turn away from your own flesh
and blood[.]
Then your light will break forth like the dawn,
    and your healing will quickly appear;
then your righteousness will go before you,
    and the glory of the Lord will be your read guard.

Isaiah 58:7-8

*God is not unjust; he will not forget your work and
the love you have shown him as you have helped
his people and continue to help them.*

Hebrews 6:10

*This service that you perform is not only supplying
the needs of God's people but is also overflowing
in many expressions of thanks to God.*

2 Corinthians 9:12

Do not withhold good from those who deserve it,
    when it is in your power to act.

Proverbs 3:27

ASSISTING OTHERS

He who is kind to the poor lends to the Lord,
   and he will reward him for what he has done.

Proverbs 19:17

A generous man will himself be blessed,
   for he shares his food with the poor.

Proverbs 22:9

Whoever is kind to the needy honors God.

Proverbs 14:31

He who gives to the poor will lack nothing.

Proverbs 28:27

The righteous care about justice for the poor.

Proverbs 29:7

Speak up for those who cannot speak for
themselves,
   for the rights of all who are destitute.
Speak up and judge fairly;
   defend the rights of the poor and needy.

Proverbs 31:8-9

*Jesus said, "Blessed are the merciful,
   for they will be shown mercy."*

Matthew 5:7

ASSISTING OTHERS

Jesus said, "Sell your possessions and give to the poor. Provide purses for yourselves that will not wear out, a treasure in heaven that will not be exhausted, where no thief comes near and no moth destroys. For where your treasure is, there your heart will be also."

Luke 12:33-34

Jesus said, "When you give a luncheon or dinner, do not invite your friends, your brothers or relatives, or your rich neighbors; if you do, they may invite you back and so you will be repaid. But when you give a banquet, invite the poor, the crippled, the lame, the blind, and you will be blessed. Although they cannot repay you, you will be repaid at the resurrection of the righteous."

Luke 14:12-14

Blessed is he who is kind to the needy.

Proverbs 14:21

Your prayers and gifts to the poor have come up as a memorial offering before God.

Acts 10:4

If I give all I possess to the poor and surrender my body to the flames, but have not love, I gain nothing.

1 Corinthians 13:3

ASSISTING OTHERS

Whoever sows generously will also reap generously. Each man should give what he has decided in his heart to give, not reluctantly or under compulsion, for God loves a cheerful giver.

2 Corinthians 9:6-7

Jesus said, "Give, and it will be given to you. A good measure, pressed down, shaken together and running over, will be poured into your lap. For with the measure you use, it will be measured to you."

Luke 6:38

The Spirit of the Sovereign LORD is on me,
    because the LORD has anointed me
    to preach good news to the poor.
He has sent me to bind up the brokenhearted,
    to proclaim freedom for the captives
    and release from darkness for the prisoners, ...
to comfort all who mourn,
    and provide for those who grieve.

Isaiah 61:1-3

ASSISTING OTHERS

David Robinson, who helped lead his team to the NBA title in 1999 and 2003, has given millions of dollars to programs that help needy kids in the San Antonio area. Calbert Chaney, who was the NCAA Player of the Year in college basketball before starting his NBA career, gave a quarter of a million dollars to his church to build a youth center.

Nehemiah heard the cries of the people who were struggling to make ends meet (Nehemiah 5). They were fighting the combined difficulties of famine and high taxes, and there was often not enough food to go around.

Those troubles touched Nehemiah's heart, and he took action. This is not always the case with leaders. Remember the disdain with which Rehoboam treated his people when they complained about similar difficulties (see 2 Chronicles 10)?

Leaders, like athletes, come with hearts that respond in various ways to the outcries of the needy. Some help; some don't.

Where do you stand? Do you see the needs of the poor and figure there's nothing you can do to fix it, so why bother?

Follow the example of David Robinson, Calbert Chaney and Nehemiah. Listen with your heart and respond out of the abundance of your resources. Give back so that others may experience the love of Christ.

AUTHORITY

To the only God our Savior be glory, majesty, power and authority, through Jesus Christ our Lord, before all ages, now and forevermore! Amen.

Jude 25

God raised Christ from the dead and seated him at his right hand in the heavenly realms, far above all rule and authority, power and dominion, and every title that can be given, not only in the present age but also in the one to come.

Ephesians 1:20-21

Jesus said, "All authority in heaven and on earth has been given to me."

Matthew 28:18

God exalted him to the highest place
   and gave him the name that is above every name,
that at the name of Jesus every knee should bow,
   in heaven and on earth and under the earth,
and every tongue confess that Jesus Christ is Lord,
   to the glory of God the Father.

Philippians 2:9-11

AUTHORITY

Everyone must submit himself to the governing authorities, for there is no authority except that which God has established. The authorities that exist have been established by God.

Romans 13:1

Submit yourselves for the Lord's sake to every authority instituted among men: whether to the king, as the supreme authority, or to governors, who are sent by him to punish those who do wrong and to commend those who do right.

1 Peter 2:13-14

Rulers hold no terror for those who do right, but for those who do wrong. Do you want to be free from fear of the one in authority? Then do what is right and he will commend you. For he is God's servant to do you good.

Romans 13:3-4

Obey your leaders and submit to their authority. They keep watch over you as men who must give an account. Obey them so that their work will be a joy, not a burden, for that would be of no advantage to you.

Hebrews 13:17

AUTHORITY

I urge ... that requests, prayers, intercession and thanksgiving be made for everyone—for kings and all those in authority, that we may live peaceful and quiet lives in all godliness and holiness.

1 Timothy 2:1-2

Respect those who work hard among you, who are over you in the Lord and who admonish you. Hold them in the highest regard in love because of their work.

1 Thessalonians 5:12-13

Jesus said, "You know that the rulers of the Gentiles lord it over them, and their high officials exercise authority over them. Not so with you. Instead, whoever wants to become great among you must be your servant, and whoever wants to be first must be your slave—just as the Son of Man did not come to be served, but to serve."

Matthew 20:25-28

I, wisdom, dwell together with prudence;
    I possess knowledge and discretion....
By me kings reign
    and rulers make laws that are just.

Proverbs 8:12, 15

AUTHORITY

Paul knew that the instructions he was about to give the Thessalonians wouldn't hold much weight with them—we're so often skeptical of those in authority—so Paul told the people his guidelines came "by the authority of the Lord Jesus" (1 Thessalonians 4:2).

Indeed, we need to know who is behind the instructions we hear so that we'll have the right attitude toward those over us.

Rhonda Blades was a guard for the Vanderbilt University Women's basketball team. Later she played for the New York Liberty and the Detroit Shock in the WNBA. She gives this advice for relating to those in authority, which is helpful to us as we obey both God and the human authority God has placed in our lives:

Be consistent

Set an example for others

Pray

Develop a strong spiritual foundation

Be a light to others

If Jesus Christ is the authority, we know what to do in response to his words of instruction: obey immediately! But for the human authority in our lives, we can keep a positive attitude and honor God by responding to that authority with respect.

CONDUCT ON THE COURT

Even a child is known by his actions,
   by whether his conduct is pure and right.

Proverbs 20:11

I will show you my faith by what I do.

James 2:18

Jesus said, "You are the light of the world. A city on a hill cannot be hidden. Neither do people light a lamp and put it under a bowl. Instead they put it on its stand, and it gives light to everyone in the house. In the same way, let your light shine before men, that they may see your good deeds and praise your Father in heaven."

Matthew 5:14-16

Each one should test his own actions.

Galatians 6:4

Who is wise and understanding among you? Let him show it by his good life, by deeds done in the humility that comes from wisdom.

James 3:13

LORD, who may dwell in your sanctuary?
   Who may live on your holy hill?
He whose walk is blameless
   and who does what is righteous.

Psalm 15:1-2

CONDUCT ON THE COURT

A fool finds pleasure in evil conduct,
  but a man of understanding delights in wisdom.

Proverbs 10:23

The prospect of the righteous is joy.

Proverbs 10:28

Jesus said, "Whoever lives by the truth comes into the light, so that it may be seen plainly that what he has done has been done through God."

John 3:21

Jesus said, "Wisdom is proved right by her actions."

Matthew 11:19

Jesus said, "I am he who searches hearts and minds, and I will repay each of you according to your deeds."

Revelation 2:23

The path of the righteous is like the first gleam of dawn,
  shining ever brighter till the full light of day.

Proverbs 4:18

CONDUCT ON THE COURT

"I the LORD search the heart
   and examine the mind,
to reward a man according to his conduct,
   according to what his deeds deserve."

Jeremiah 17:10

The LORD is a God who knows,
   and by him deeds are weighed.

1 Samuel 2:3

"My eyes will be on the faithful in the land,
   that they may dwell with me;
he whose walk is blameless
   will minister to me,"
      declares the LORD.

Psalm 101:6

*"I will judge you according to your conduct,"
declares the LORD.*

Ezekiel 7:3

God will bring every deed into judgment,
   including every hidden thing,
   whether it is good or evil.

Ecclesiastes 12:14

CONDUCT ON THE COURT

Tell the righteous it will be well with them,
 for they will enjoy the fruit of their deeds.

Isaiah 3:10

The noble man makes noble plans,
 and by noble deeds he stands.

Isaiah 32:8

As you have done, it will be done to you;
 your deeds will return upon your own head.

Obadiah 15

*They should repent and turn to God and prove
their repentance by their deeds.*

Acts 26:20

*Command those who are rich in this present world
not to be arrogant nor to put their hope in wealth,
which is so uncertain, but to put their hope in God,
who richly provides us with everything for our
enjoyment. Command them to do good, to be
rich in good deeds, and to be generous and willing
to share.*

1 Timothy 6:17-18

CONDUCT ON THE COURT

The conduct of the innocent is upright.

Proverbs 21:8

The night is nearly over; the day is almost here. So let us put aside the deeds of darkness and put on the armor of light. Let us behave decently, as in the daytime.

Romans 13:12-13

Since we live by the Spirit, let us keep in step with the Spirit.

Galatians 5:25

Let us not love with words or tongue but with actions and in truth.

1 John 3:18

Good deeds are obvious, and even those that are not cannot be hidden.

1 Timothy 5:25

Jesus said, "The righteous will shine like the sun in the kingdom of their Father."

Matthew 13:43

His faith and his actions were working together, and his faith was made complete by what he did.

James 2:22

CONDUCT ON THE COURT

There on the front of sports' most famous magazine was David Robinson with the title "Saint David" emblazoned across his photo. Inside the April 29, 1996, edition of the magazine was this subtitle: "San Antonio Spurs center and born-again Christian David Robinson is trying to lead his team to an NBA title and remain pure in a world beset by the seven deadly sins."

It was a remarkable article because it allowed the reader to understand how one man could truly live by ideals such as those Paul presented in Philippians 1:27: "Whatever happens, conduct yourselves in a manner worthy of the gospel of Christ."

No, David Robinson was not, and is not, perfect. Neither was Paul. And neither are we. But that does not excuse us from this wonderful opportunity that the apostle describes. We can, with the Holy Spirit's help and with godly determination, live in a way that reflects well on our Savior and on the gospel he died to give us.

It's an error to think we have to have a platform such as being the MVP of the NBA in order to make a difference for Christ. Each of us, by conducting ourselves with care, with honor and with an eye toward living in a Christlike way, can walk in a manner worthy of the gospel.

CONFLICT

Jesus said, "You have heard that it was said, 'Eye for eye, and tooth for tooth.' But I tell you, Do not resist an evil person. If someone strikes you on the right cheek, turn to him the other also."

Matthew 5:38-39

If any of you has a dispute with another, dare he take it before the ungodly for judgment instead of before the saints? Do you not know that the saints will judge the world? And if you are to judge the world, are you not competent to judge trivial cases? Do you not know that we will judge angels? How much more the things of this life! Therefore, if you have disputes about such matters, appoint as judges even men of little account in the church!

1 Corinthians 6:1-4

It is to a man's honor to avoid strife.

Proverbs 20:3

The Lord's servant must not quarrel; instead, he must be kind to everyone, able to teach, not resentful. Those who oppose him he must gently instruct, in the hope that God will grant them repentance leading them to a knowledge of the truth.

2 Timothy 2:24-25

CONFLICT

Jesus said, "If someone wants to sue you and take your tunic, let him have your cloak as well."

Matthew 5:40

The wisdom that comes from heaven is first of all pure; then peace-loving, considerate, submissive, full of mercy and good fruit, impartial and sincere.

James 3:17

Jesus said, "Settle matters quickly with your adversary who is taking you to court."

Matthew 5:25

Be completely humble and gentle; be patient, bearing with one another in love.

Ephesians 4:2

Let the peace of Christ rule in your hearts, since as members of one body you were called to peace.

Colossians 3:15

A patient man calms a quarrel.

Proverbs 15:18

CONFLICT

Better a dry crust with peace and quiet
than a house full of feasting, with strife.

Proverbs 17:1

*We were harassed at every turn—conflicts on the
outside, fears within. But God, who comforts the
downcast, comforted us.*

2 Corinthians 7:5

Without wood a fire goes out;
without gossip a quarrel dies down.
As charcoal to embers and as wood to fire,
so is a quarrelsome man for kindling strife.

Proverbs 26:20-21

*Do everything without complaining or arguing, so
that you may become blameless and pure, children
of God without fault in a crooked and depraved
generation, in which you shine like stars in the universe as you hold out the word of life.*

Philippians 2:14-16

Drive out the mocker, and out goes strife;
quarrels and insults are ended.

Proverbs 22:10

CONFLICT

Starting a quarrel is like breaching a dam;
  so drop the matter before a dispute breaks out.

Proverbs 17:14

*Abram said to Lot, "Let's not have any quarreling
between you and me, or between your herdsmen
and mine, for we are brothers."*

Genesis 13:8

*Don't have anything to do with foolish and stupid
arguments, because you know they produce quarrels.*

2 Timothy 2:23

*What causes fights and quarrels among you?
Don't they come from your desires that battle
within you? You want something but don't get it.
You kill and covet, but you cannot have what you
want. You quarrel and fight. You do not have,
because you do not ask God. When you ask, you
do not receive, because you ask with wrong
motives, that you may spend what you get on your
pleasures.*

James 4:1-3

CONFLICT

Jesus said, "If someone forces you to go one mile, go with him two miles."

Matthew 5:41

Peacemakers who sow in peace raise a harvest of righteousness.

James 3:18

Do not take revenge, my friends, but leave room for God's wrath, for it is written: "It is mine to avenge; I will repay," says the Lord.

Romans 12:19

Turn from evil and do good;
seek peace and pursue it.

Psalm 34:14

Make every effort to keep the unity of the Spirit through the bond of peace.

Ephesians 4:3

How good and pleasant it is
when brothers live together in unity!

Psalm 133:1

CONFLICT

If you want to talk about a change of plans in sports, you can start right up there at the top. Michael Jordan has changed his plans so often you almost need a chart to keep up.

1. He announced that he was retiring from basketball, leaving the impression that he was done with pro athletics.

2. He changed his mind and joined up with the Chicago White Sox organization as a baseball player.

3. When that move didn't lead to a promotion from the minor leagues to Comiskey Park, he retired from baseball.

4. He "unretired" from basketball, whipped himself back into hoops shape and won some more titles.

When the apostle Paul wrote to the people at Corinth, he apologized to them for his change in plans (2 Corinthians).

These changes created some unrest in Corinth, and Paul wanted to calm that situation. He told them that he had decided not to come to Corinth in order to spare them the disciplinary action that would have been a part of his visit. He was not eager for a battle.

We, too, can avoid trouble by providing alternatives to conflict. Paul's change of plans underlines his desire to avoid unnecessary trouble.

DEDICATION

Jesus said, "Love the Lord your God with all your heart and with all your soul and with all your mind and with all your strength."

Mark 12:30

What does the LORD your God ask of you but to fear the LORD your God, to walk in all his ways, to love him, to serve the LORD your God with all your heart and with all your soul, and to observe the LORD's commands and decrees?

Deuteronomy 10:12-13

He has showed you, O man, what is good.
  And what does the LORD require of you?
To act justly and to love mercy
  and to walk humbly with your God.

Micah 6:8

This is what Hezekiah did throughout Judah, doing what was good and right and faithful before the LORD his God. In everything that he undertook in the service of God's temple and in obedience to the law and the commands, he sought his God and worked wholeheartedly. And so he prospered.

2 Chronicles 31:20-21

"You will seek me and find me when you seek me with all your heart. I will be found by you," declares the LORD.

Jeremiah 29:13-14

DEDICATION

Whatever you do, work at it with all your heart, as working for the Lord, not for men, since you know that you will receive an inheritance from the Lord as a reward. It is the Lord Christ you are serving.

Colossians 3:23-24

You must serve faithfully and wholeheartedly in the fear of the LORD.

2 Chronicles 19:9

Remember, O LORD, how I have walked before you faithfully and with wholehearted devotion and have done what is good in your eyes.

2 Kings 20:3

Acknowledge the God of your father, and serve him with wholehearted devotion and with a willing mind, for the LORD searches every heart and understands every motive behind the thoughts.

1 Chronicles 28:9

"I remember the devotion of your youth,
    how as a bride you loved me
and followed me through the desert,
    through a land not sown,"
        declares the LORD.

Jeremiah 2:2

DEDICATION

Be very careful to keep the commandment and the law that Moses the servant of the LORD gave you: to love the LORD your God, to walk in all his ways, to obey his commands, to hold fast to him and to serve him with all your heart and all your soul.

Joshua 22:5

Serve wholeheartedly, as if you were serving the Lord, not men, because you know that the Lord will reward everyone for whatever good he does.

Ephesians 6:7-8

Live in a right way in undivided devotion to the Lord.

1 Corinthians 7:35

O LORD, God of Israel, there is no God like you in heaven above or on earth below—you who keep your covenant of love with your servants who continue wholeheartedly in your way.

1 Kings 8:23

Choose for yourselves this day whom you will serve.... But as for me and my household, we will serve the LORD.

Joshua 24:15

DEDICATION

During my career as a high school basketball coach, I never asked my players to give me 110 percent. I was pretty happy if I got anything that resembled 100 percent, and I didn't think it would be too wise to ask them for something they couldn't give me.

You see, I don't think you can give 110 percent. It's a physical impossibility. I suppose it might sound good in a pregame speech: "Give it all you've got and more! Now go out and win, win, win!"

Not even God would ask for that. Look at how David implored his son Solomon when he gave him a pep talk: "Acknowledge the God of your father, and serve him with wholehearted devotion and with a willing mind, for the LORD searches every heart and understands every motive" (1 Chronicles 28:9).

Notice what David called for: "wholehearted devotion." That means giving 100 percent. Not more. Not less.

God is reasonable. He knows our hearts and our motives, and if we are giving him our "wholehearted devotion," he'll bless us, encourage us and strengthen us.

Does giving 110 percent sound impossible? It is.

All God wants is 100 percent. He wants our devotion and our love. And he deserves it a lot more than a coach does, even a great coach.

DEFENSE

Be self-controlled and alert. Your enemy the devil prowls around like a roaring lion looking for someone to devour. Resist him, standing firm in the faith.

1 Peter 5:8-9

If you do not do what is right, sin is crouching at your door; it desires to have you, but you must master it.

Genesis 4:7

Be strong in the Lord and in his mighty power. Put on the full armor of God so that you can take your stand against the devil's schemes. For our struggle is not against flesh and blood, but against the rulers, against the authorities, against the powers of this dark world and against the spiritual forces of evil in the heavenly realms.

Ephesians 6:10-12

Jesus said, "Watch and pray so that you will not fall into temptation."

Matthew 26:41

If you think you are standing firm, be careful that you don't fall!

1 Corinthians 10:12

DEFENSE

Jesus said, "Pray that you will not fall into temptation."

Luke 22:40

Resist the devil, and he will flee from you.

James 4:7

Because Jesus himself suffered when he was tempted, he is able to help those who are being tempted.

Hebrews 2:18

Flee the evil desires of youth, and pursue righteousness, faith, love and peace, along with those who call on the Lord out of a pure heart.

2 Timothy 2:22

Since we have a great high priest who has gone through the heavens, Jesus the Son of God, let us hold firmly to the faith we profess. For we do not have a high priest who is unable to sympathize with our weaknesses, but we have one who has been tempted in every way, just as we are—yet was without sin.

Hebrews 4:14-15

DEFENSE

Jesus was led by the Spirit into the desert to be tempted by the devil. After fasting forty days and forty nights, he was hungry. The tempter came to him and said, "If you are the Son of God, tell these stones to become bread." Jesus answered, "It is written: 'Man does not live on bread alone, but on every word that comes from the mouth of God.'"

Matthew 4:1-4

When tempted, no one should say, "God is tempting me." For God cannot be tempted by evil, nor does he tempt anyone; but each one is tempted when, by his own evil desire, he is dragged away and enticed. Then, after desire has conceived, it gives birth to sin; and sin, when it is full-grown, gives birth to death.

James 1:13-15

The Spirit helps us in our weakness. We do not know what we ought to pray for, but the Spirit himself intercedes for us with groans that words cannot express. And he who searches our hearts knows the mind of the Spirit, because the Spirit intercedes for the saints in accordance with God's will.

Romans 8:26-27

DEFENSE

No temptation has seized you except what is common to man. And God is faithful; he will not let you be tempted beyond what you can bear. But when you are tempted, he will also provide a way out so that you can stand up under it.

1 Corinthians 10:13

The love of money is a root of all kinds of evil. Some people, eager for money, have wandered from the faith and pierced themselves with many griefs. But you, man of God, flee from all this, and pursue righteousness, godliness, faith, love, endurance and gentleness. Fight the good fight of the faith.

1 Timothy 6:10-12

Put on the full armor of God, so that when the day of evil comes, you may be able to stand your ground, and after you have done everything, to stand. Stand firm then, with the belt of truth buckled around your waist, with the breastplate of righteousness in place, and with your feet fitted with the readiness that comes from the gospel of peace. In addition to all this, take up the shield of faith, with which you can extinguish all the flaming arrows of the evil one. Take the helmet of salvation and the sword of the Spirit, which is the word of God.

Ephesians 6:13-17

DEFENSE

Who will bring any charge against those whom God has chosen? It is God who justifies. Who is he that condemns? Christ Jesus, who died—more than that, who was raised to life—is at the right hand of God and is also interceding for us.

Romans 8:33-34

Because the Sovereign LORD helps me,
    I will not be disgraced.
Therefore have I set my face like flint,
    and I know I will not be put to shame.
He who vindicates me is near.
    Who then will bring charges against me?
    Let us face each other!
Who is my accuser?
    Let him confront me!
It is the Sovereign LORD who helps me.

Isaiah 50:7-9

Now have come the salvation and the power
and the kingdom of our God,
    and the authority of his Christ.
For the accuser of our brothers,
    who accuses them before our God day and
night,
    has been hurled down.
They overcame him
    by the blood of the Lamb
    and by the word of their testimony.

Revelation 12:10-11

DEFENSE

To my way of thinking, there's nothing better than a good trapping defense to stop a basketball team. The key, though, is to lure a ball handler into the trap, where he or she is defended by two people while all passing lanes are shut down.

As a coach, I tried to get my trapping players to let a guard get the ball just past half-court and then clamp on the trap and make the player pick up his or her dribble. For many guards, panic sets in when they realize how few options are available.

Old Elijah set up a pretty good trapping defense of his own when he was trying to capture the Arameans (2 Kings 6:8-23). With a lot of help from God, Elijah led the enemy inside the walls of Samaria. Once they saw where they were and what their options were, they knew they had been defeated.

How good and wise it is for us to trust God when we are under attack—and we all face attacks of various kinds in our lives. God has given us his Spirit for guidance and his Word for direction. That's all we need to defeat our enemy and please God.

We may not use an Elijah-like trap, but we know we can win with a God-directed defense.

ETERNAL LIFE

The wages of sin is death, but the gift of God is eternal life in Christ Jesus our Lord.

Romans 6:23

Jesus said, "I tell you the truth, whoever hears my word and believes him who sent me has eternal life and will not be condemned; he has crossed over from death to life."

John 5:24

Everyone who calls
   on the name of the Lord will be saved.

Acts 2:21

The one who sows to please the Spirit, from the Spirit will reap eternal life.

Galatians 6:8

Jesus said, "Now this is eternal life: that they may know you, the only true God, and Jesus Christ, whom you have sent."

John 17:3

God "will give to each person according to what he has done." To those who by persistence in doing good seek glory, honor and immortality, he will give eternal life.

Romans 2:6-7

ETERNAL LIFE

Jesus said, *"God so loved the world that he gave his one and only Son, that whoever believes in him shall not perish but have eternal life."*

John 3:16

Jesus said, *"I am the bread of life.... I am the living bread that came down from heaven. If anyone eats of this bread, he will live forever."*

John 6:48, 51

Jesus Christ is the true God and eternal life.

1 John 5:20

Believe in the Lord Jesus, and you will be saved.

Acts 16:31

The world and its desires pass away, but the man who does the will of God lives forever.

1 John 2:17

Jesus said, *"My sheep listen to my voice; I know them, and they follow me. I give them eternal life, and they shall never perish; no one can snatch them out of my hand."*

John 10:27-28

ETERNAL LIFE

Repent and be baptized, every one of you, in the name of Jesus Christ for the forgiveness of your sins. And you will receive the gift of the Holy Spirit.

Acts 2:38

It is by grace you have been saved, through faith— and this not from yourselves, it is the gift of God.

Ephesians 2:8

Jesus said, "My Father's will is that everyone who looks to the Son and believes in him shall have eternal life, and I will raise him up at the last day."

John 6:40

God has given us eternal life, and this life is in his Son. He who has the Son has life.

1 John 5:11-12

Many of Jesus' disciples turned back and no longer followed him. "You do not want to leave too, do you?" Jesus asked the Twelve. Simon Peter answered him, "Lord, to whom shall we go? You have the words of eternal life. We believe and know that you are the Holy One of God."

John 6:66-69

ETERNAL LIFE

There are some lists in sports from which the names are never removed.

For instance, I opened up the Houston Rockets all-time roster and noticed the following names listed: Bud Acton, Harry Barnes, Joe Bryant, Mike Dunleavy, Pat Riley. Nearly 200 NBA players have played on that team at one time or another and their names will never be erased from the list.

In the book of Revelation, we discover another book that has a list that cannot be altered. It's a book that has a list of everyone who, through faith in Jesus Christ, will be allowed to enter God's kingdom of eternal joy. In Revelation 3:5, we read Jesus' reference to the book in his message to the church in Sardis. He said, "He who overcomes will, like them, be dressed in white. I will never blot out his name from the book of life."

Now we're talking permanent ink!

Once a Houston Rocket, always a Houston Rocket. That sounds pretty good for Harry Barnes. But I like the sound of once a Christian, always a Christian.

No matter what lists you've been on before—even if it is one of the most prestigious lists humans can put together—please make sure you are also listed in the Lamb's book of life.

FAITH

The righteous will live by faith.

Romans 1:17

Jesus said, "I tell you the truth, if you have faith and do not doubt ... you can say to this mountain, 'Go, throw yourself into the sea,' and it will be done. If you believe, you will receive whatever you ask for in prayer."

Matthew 21:21-22

Faith is being sure of what we hope for and certain of what we do not see.

Hebrews 11:1

Everyone born of God overcomes the world. This is the victory that has overcome the world, even our faith. Who is it that overcomes the world? Only he who believes that Jesus is the Son of God.

1 John 5:4-5

I lift up my eyes to the hills—
    where does my help come from?
My help comes from the LORD,
    the Maker of heaven and earth.

Psalm 121:1-2

FAITH

We live by faith, not by sight.

2 Corinthians 5:7

"Fear not, for I have redeemed you;
I have summoned you by name; you are mine.
When you pass through the waters,
I will be with you;
and when you pass through the rivers,
they will not sweep over you.
When you walk through the fire,
you will not be burned;
the flames will not set you ablaze,"
declares the LORD.

Isaiah 43:1-2

The LORD watches over you—
the LORD is your shade at your right hand;
the sun will not harm you by day,
nor the moon by night.

Psalm 121:5-6

Without faith it is impossible to please God,
because anyone who comes to him must believe
that he exists and that he rewards those who
earnestly seek him.

Hebrews 11:6

FAITH

Have faith in the LORD your God and you will be upheld.

2 Chronicles 20:20

Love the LORD, all his saints!
    The LORD preserves the faithful....
Be strong and take heart,
    all you who hope in the LORD.

Psalm 31:23-24

O LORD, you preserve both man and beast.
    How priceless is your unfailing love!
Both high and low among men
    find refuge in the shadow of your wings.

Psalm 36:6-7

The LORD loves the just
    and will not forsake his faithful ones.
They will be protected forever.

Psalm 37:28

Love and faithfulness meet together;
    righteousness and peace kiss each other.
Faithfulness springs forth from the earth,
    and righteousness looks down from heaven.

Psalm 85:10-11

FAITH

Let those who love the LORD hate evil,
  for he guards the lives of his faithful ones
  and delivers them from the hand of the wicked.
Light is shed upon the righteous
  and joy on the upright in heart.

Psalm 97:10-11

The LORD is faithful to all his promises
  and loving toward all he has made.
The LORD upholds all those who fall
  and lifts up all who are bowed down.
The eyes of all look to you,
  and you give them their food at the proper time.
You open your hand
  and satisfy the desires of every living thing.

Psalm 145:13-16

Let love and faithfulness never leave you;
  bind them around your neck,
  write them on the tablet of your heart.
Then you will win favor and a good name
  in the sight of God and man.

Proverbs 3:3-4

FAITH

Let us throw off everything that hinders and the sin that so easily entangles, and let us run with perseverance the race marked out for us. Let us fix our eyes on Jesus, the author and perfecter of our faith, who for the joy set before him endured the cross, scorning its shame, and sat down at the right hand of the throne of God.

Hebrews 12:1-2

Do not fear, for I am with you;
do not be dismayed, for I am your God.
I will strengthen you and help you;
I will uphold you with my righteous right hand.

Isaiah 41:10

If God is for us, who can be against us?

Romans 8:31

What more shall I say? I do not have time to tell about Gideon, Barak, Samson, Jephthah, David, Samuel and the prophets, who through faith conquered kingdoms, administered justice, and gained what was promised; who shut the mouths of lions, quenched the fury of the flames, and escaped the edge of the sword; whose weakness was turned to strength; and who became powerful in battle and routed foreign armies.

Hebrews 11:32-34

FAITH

Gideon's army was like Allen Iverson—but without the tattoos. Out-manned, outsized, out-every-thinged.

The Midianites were like Shaquille O'Neal. Impenetrable. Unmovable. Unstoppable.

Yet even little Allen Iverson conquered the mighty Shaq from time to time. For "The Answer," it took courage, brains, fortitude and sheer willpower.

For Gideon's army it took faith.

How many times do we face Shaq-like foes in life?

Perhaps there's an addiction that looks over 7 feet tall. Or maybe it's a physical ailment that appears to weigh about 300 pounds. And here we are with our tiny 6-foot faith, wondering how we can ever take home a victory.

"The Answer" in this case is not Allen Iverson. It's Gideon. Here's what he did (Judges 6):

- He obeyed God's orders. Surely we too can know from Scripture how God wants us to live.

- He worshipped God. Indeed we need to acknowledge that God is greater than any problem.

- He led the way in faith and action. We say we believe, but how often do we prove our faith by what we do?

Are we going to let the big problems in our life win again? Not this time. With God on our side, we're unstoppable.

FAVORITISM

God does not show favoritism but accepts men from every nation who fear him and do what is right.

Acts 10:34-35

With the L ORD our God there is no injustice or partiality.

2 Chronicles 19:7

Is he not the One …
who shows no partiality to princes
 and does not favor the rich over the poor,
 for they are all the work of his hands?

Job 34:18-19

The L ORD your God is God of gods and Lord of lords, the great God, mighty and awesome, who shows no partiality and accepts no bribes. He defends the cause of the fatherless and the widow, and loves the alien, giving him food and clothing.

Deuteronomy 10:17-18

The L ORD does not look at the things man looks at. Man looks at the outward appearance, but the L ORD looks at the heart.

1 Samuel 16:7

FAVORITISM

As believers in our glorious Lord Jesus Christ, don't show favoritism. Suppose a man comes into your meeting wearing a gold ring and fine clothes, and a poor man in shabby clothes also comes in. If you show special attention to the man wearing fine clothes and say, "Here's a good seat for you," but say to the poor man, "You stand there" or "Sit on the floor by my feet," have you not discriminated among yourselves and become judges with evil thoughts? ... Has not God chosen those who are poor in the eyes of the world to be rich in faith and to inherit the kingdom he promised those who love him?

James 2:1-5

Jesus, we know that you speak and teach what is right, and that you do not show partiality but teach the way of God in accordance with the truth.

Luke 20:21

Do not show partiality to the poor or favoritism to the great, but judge your neighbor fairly.

Leviticus 19:15

To show partiality is not good.

Proverbs 28:21

If a king judges the poor with fairness,
    his throne will always be secure.

Proverbs 29:14

FAVORITISM

Anyone who does wrong will be repaid for his wrong, and there is no favoritism.

Colossians 3:25

If you really keep the royal law found in Scripture, "Love your neighbor as yourself," you are doing right. But if you show favoritism, you sin and are convicted by the law.

James 2:8-9

Suppose there is a righteous man
    who does what is just and right....
He withholds his hand from doing wrong
    and judges fairly between man and man....
That man is righteous;
    he will surely live,
    declares the Sovereign LORD.

Ezekiel 18:5, 8-9

It is not good to be partial to the wicked
    or to deprive the innocent of justice.

Proverbs 18:5

I charge you, in the sight of God and Christ Jesus and the elect angels, to keep these instructions without partiality, and to do nothing out of favoritism.

1 Timothy 5:21

FAVORITISM

I have been to the top of the Palace of Auburn Hills, home for many years to the Detroit Pistons, and I tell you no lies, it's not a good place from which to watch a basketball game. You feel no connection to the action when the players are way, way down there.

I've also had the opportunity to sit at press row in the same arena—up close, where you can smell the stuff the players rub on their sore muscles. From your vantage point three feet from the playing floor, it's easy to look up at those unfortunate fans who are populating the seats nearest heaven and feel sorry for them. It's hard to consider those folks as equals.

James knew that good seats and bad seats can indicate a difference in perceived importance. He knew that if a person came into a church and didn't look right, he or she could be relegated to the "cheap seats" and made to feel less important than the wealthy-looking people in the front rows.

God hates it when we treat one person as if he or she were better than another. James 2:1 says, "Don't show favoritism"—in the church, in the family, in life.

The "Jack Nicholson seats" in our churches should be open to everybody. And so should our arms.

FOLLOWING JESUS

As Jesus was walking beside the Sea of Galilee, he saw two brothers, Simon called Peter and his brother Andrew. They were casting a net into the lake, for they were fishermen. "Come, follow me," Jesus said, "and I will make you fishers of men." At once they left their nets and followed him…He saw two other brothers, James son of Zebedee and his brother John. They were in a boat with their father Zebedee, preparing their nets. Jesus called them, and immediately they left the boat and their father and followed him.

Matthew 4:18-22

Jesus went out and saw a tax collector by the name of Levi sitting at his tax booth. "Follow me," Jesus said to him, and Levi got up, left everything and followed him.

Luke 5:27-28

"I tell you the truth," Jesus said, "no one who has left home or brothers or sisters or mother or father or children or fields for me and the gospel will fail to receive a hundred times as much in this present age … and in the age to come, eternal life."

Mark 10:29-30

FOLLOWING JESUS

Jesus said to another man, "Follow me." But the man replied, "Lord, first let me go and bury my father." Jesus said to him, "Let the dead bury their own dead, but you go and proclaim the kingdom of God."

Luke 9:59-60

Jesus said, "Whoever serves me must follow me; and where I am, my servant also will be. My Father will honor the one who serves me."

John 12:26

The LORD is my shepherd, I shall not be in want.
     He makes me lie down in green pastures,
he leads me beside quiet waters,
     he restores my soul.
He guides me in paths of righteousness
     for his name's sake.
Even though I walk
     through the valley of the shadow of death,
I will fear no evil,
     for you are with me;
your rod and your staff,
     they comfort me.

Psalm 23:1-4

FOLLOWING JESUS

When Jesus had finished washing their feet, he put on his clothes and returned to his place. "Do you understand what I have done for you?" he asked them. "You call me 'Teacher' and 'Lord,' and rightly so, for that is what I am. Now that I, your Lord and Teacher, have washed your feet, you also should wash one another's feet. I have set you an example that you should do as I have done for you."

John 13:12-15

Jesus said, "Enter through the narrow gate. For wide is the gate and broad is the road that leads to destruction, and many enter through it. But small is the gate and narrow the road that leads to life, and only a few find it."

Matthew 7:13-14

Jesus said, "Not everyone who says to me, 'Lord, Lord,' will enter the kingdom of heaven, but only he who does the will of my Father who is in heaven."

Matthew 7:21

Jesus said, "If you want to be perfect, go, sell your possessions and give to the poor, and you will have treasure in heaven. Then come, follow me."

Matthew 19:21

FOLLOWING JESUS

Jesus said to his disciples, "I tell you the truth, it is hard for a rich man to enter the kingdom of heaven. Again I tell you, it is easier for a camel to go through the eye of a needle than for a rich man to enter the kingdom of God." When the disciples heard this, they were greatly astonished and asked, "Who then can be saved?" Jesus looked at them and said, "With man this is impossible, but with God all things are possible."

Matthew 19:23-26

Jesus said to his disciples, "If anyone would come after me, he must deny himself and take up his cross and follow me. For whoever wants to save his life will lose it, but whoever loses his life for me will find it."

Matthew 16:24-25

Jesus said, "Whoever serves me must follow me; and where I am, my servant also will be. My Father will honor the one who serves me."

John 12:26

Jesus said, "I am the light of the world. Whoever follows me will never walk in darkness, but will have the light of life."

John 8:12

FOLLOWING JESUS

Jesus said, "The man who enters by the gate is the shepherd of his sheep. The watchman opens the gate for him, and the sheep listen to his voice. He calls his own sheep by name and leads them out. When he has brought out all his own, he goes on ahead of them, and his sheep follow him because they know his voice.... I am the good shepherd; I know my sheep and my sheep know me."

John 10:2, 14

Still another said, "I will follow you, Lord; but first let me go back and say good-by to my family." Jesus replied, "No one who puts his hand to the plow and looks back is fit for service in the kingdom of God."

Luke 9:61-62

Jesus said, "Suppose one of you wants to build a tower. Will he not first sit down and estimate the cost to see if he has enough money to complete it? ... In the same way, any of you who does not give up everything he has cannot be my disciple."

Luke 14:28, 33

FOLLOWING JESUS

Of all the recorded words of Jesus, one of the most heart-rending phrases is recorded in John 6.

Jesus had spoken some words that were probably misunderstood by some of his followers. Jesus recognized that some people would not be able to listen to those words and continue with him. John 6:66 records that what Jesus anticipated did indeed happen: "From this time many of his disciples turned back and no longer followed him."

Then Jesus asks those who remained with him: "You do not want to leave too, do you?" (John 6:67). We can read into those words the heart-breaking grief Jesus must have felt at losing some of those who had set out at first to follow him.

But imagine how he would feel if someone came along to follow Jesus to replace one of the fair-weather followers. He would rejoice! That's how he must have felt when Dana Lau gave her life to Christ.

Lau played college basketball for Northern Illinois University in the mid-nineties. She was an affirmed atheist when she began attending college. But some of the women on her team were Christians, and through their caring actions and perseverance, Lau came to Christ.

Lau is a contrast to the "fair-weather followers" who turned away from Jesus when the circumstances got difficult. When she became one of his followers, all of heaven rejoiced!

GLORIFYING GOD

*Live such good lives among [unbelievers] that ...
they may see your good deeds and glorify God.*

1 Peter 2:12

*Be wise in the way you act toward outsiders; make
the most of every opportunity. Let your conversa-
tion be always full of grace, seasoned with salt, so
that you may know how to answer everyone.*

Colossians 4:5-6

*Because of the service by which you have proved
yourselves, men will praise God for the obedience
that accompanies your confession of the gospel of
Christ.*

2 Corinthians 9:13

*Live lives worthy of God, who calls you into his
kingdom and glory.*

1 Thessalonians 2:12

*Do you not know that your body is a temple of the
Holy Spirit, who is in you, whom you have
received from God? You are not your own; you
were bought at a price. Therefore honor God with
your body.*

1 Corinthians 6:19-20

GLORFIYING GOD

This is love for God: to obey his commands.

1 John 5:3

Never be lacking in zeal, but keep your spiritual fervor, serving the Lord.

Romans 12:11

Jesus said, "He who works for the honor of the one who sent him is a man of truth."

John 7:18

Keeping God's commands is what counts.

1 Corinthians 7:19

Whatever you do, whether in word or deed, do it all in the name of the Lord Jesus, giving thanks to God the Father through him.

Colossians 3:17

Offer your bodies as living sacrifices, holy and pleasing to God—this is your spiritual act of worship.

Romans 12:1

GLORIFYING GOD

Jesus said, "I am the vine; you are the branches. If a man remains in me and I in him, he will bear much fruit; apart from me you can do nothing. If anyone does not remain in me, he is like a branch that is thrown away and withers; such branches are picked up, thrown into the fire and burned. If you remain in me and my words remain in you, ask whatever you wish, and it will be given you. This is to my Father's glory, that you bear much fruit, showing yourselves to be my disciples."

John 15:5-8

Abraham did not waver through unbelief regarding the promise of God, but was strengthened in his faith and gave glory to God, being fully persuaded that God had power to do what he had promised.

Romans 4:20-21

It is written: "I believed; therefore I have spoken." With that same spirit of faith we also believe and therefore speak, because we know that the one who raised the Lord Jesus from the dead will also raise us with Jesus and present us with you in his presence. All this is for your benefit, so that the grace that is reaching more and more people may cause thanksgiving to overflow to the glory of God.

2 Corinthians 4:13-15

GLORIFYING GOD

This is my prayer: that your love may abound more and more in knowledge and depth of insight, so that you may be able to discern what is best and may be pure and blameless until the day of Christ, filled with the fruit of righteousness that comes through Jesus Christ—to the glory and praise of God.

Philippians 1:9-11

We constantly pray for you, that our God may count you worthy of his calling, and that by his power he may fulfill every good purpose of yours and every act prompted by your faith. We pray this so that the name of our Lord Jesus may be glorified in you, and you in him, according to the grace of our God and the Lord Jesus Christ.

2 Thessalonians 1:11-12

Jesus prayed, "Father, the time has come. Glorify your Son, that your Son may glorify you.... I have brought you glory on earth by completing the work you gave me to do."

John 17:1, 4

GLORIFYING GOD

If anyone speaks, he should do it as one speaking the very words of God. If anyone serves, he should do it with the strength God provides, so that in all things God may be praised through Jesus Christ. To him be the glory and the power for ever and ever.

1 Peter 4:11

The kingdom of God is ... a matter of ... righteousness, peace and joy in the Holy Spirit, because anyone who serves Christ in this way is pleasing to God and approved by men.

Romans 14:17-18

Fear God and give him glory.... Worship him who made the heavens, the earth, the sea and the springs of water.

Revelation 14:7

Whether you eat or drink or whatever you do, do it all for the glory of God.

1 Corinthians 10:31

GLORIFYING GOD

Nothing's more frightening than the first day of practice for an athlete joining a new team.

Imagine, for example, that a woman is asked to report to a WNBA team. She doesn't know anyone, and she doesn't know exactly what to expect.

As she talks to the others, she hears stories and tries to grasp what is important to remember and what is not essential. But she really cannot understand completely what is expected of her until she hears from the coach.

In life, we're somewhat like that player. We hear all kinds of philosophies from other people. We wonder what our duties in life might be. But until we go to the source—to God himself—we won't know anything for sure.

At the end of Ecclesiastes, the author moves from telling us about other philosophies of life to finally revealing what the "whole duty of man" (Ecclesiastes 12:13) really is. It is this: "Fear God and keep his commandments." Indeed, the task God asks of us is simple: Give him the love and reverence he deserves and the sacrifice of obedience.

Life is meaningless if we don't keep that concept in mind. All of the otherwise empty things described in Ecclesiastes take on new and valuable meaning when we participate in them for God's glory and out of obedience to him.

GOD'S CALL

I pray ... that the eyes of your heart may be enlightened in order that you may know the hope to which God has called you, the riches of his glorious inheritance in the saints, and his incomparably great power for us who believe.

Ephesians 1:18-19

You also are among those who are called to belong to Jesus Christ.

Romans 1:6

God, who has called you into fellowship with his Son Jesus Christ our Lord, is faithful.

1 Corinthians 1:9

We are God's workmanship, created in Christ Jesus to do good works, which God prepared in advance for us to do.

Ephesians 2:10

Today, if you hear God's voice,
  do not harden your hearts.

Psalm 95:7-8

GOD'S CALL

"Come, all you who are thirsty,
  come to the waters....
Give ear and come to me;
  hear me, that your soul may live,"
    declares the LORD.

Isaiah 55:1, 3

In Christ we were also chosen, having been predestined according to the plan of him who works out everything in conformity with the purpose of his will, in order that we, who were first to hope in Christ, might be for the praise of his glory.

Ephesians 1:11

We know ... that God has chosen you, because our gospel came to you not simply with words, but also with power, with the Holy Spirit and with deep conviction.

1 Thessalonians 1:4-5

"I am the LORD,
  the God of Israel, who summons you by name."

Isaiah 45:3

GOD'S CALL

Therefore, holy brothers, who share in the heavenly calling, fix your thoughts on Jesus, the apostle and high priest whom we confess.

Hebrews 3:1

God did not call us to be impure, but to live a holy life.

1 Thessalonians 4:7

Jesus saw a man named Matthew sitting at the tax collector's booth. "Follow me," he told him, and Matthew got up and followed him.

Matthew 9:9

God's gifts and his call are irrevocable.

Romans 11:29

Jesus said, "Here I am! I stand at the door and knock. If anyone hears my voice and opens the door, I will come in and eat with him, and he with me."

Revelation 3:20

Blessed are those who are invited to the wedding supper of the Lamb!

Revelation 19:9

GOD'S CALL

Christ is the mediator of a new covenant, that those who are called may receive the promised eternal inheritance.

Hebrews 9:15

From the beginning God chose you to be saved through the sanctifying work of the Spirit and through belief in the truth. He called you to this through our gospel, that you might share in the glory of our Lord Jesus Christ.

2 Thessalonians 2:13-14

Jesus said, "You do not belong to the world, but I have chosen you out of the world."

John 15:19

May God himself, the God of peace, sanctify you through and through. May your whole spirit, soul and body be kept blameless at the coming of our Lord Jesus Christ. The one who calls you is faithful and he will do it.

1 Thessalonians 5:23-24

The God of all grace ... called you to his eternal glory in Christ.

1 Peter 5:10

GOD'S CALL

To those who have been called, who are loved by God the Father and kept by Jesus Christ: Mercy, peace and love be yours in abundance.

Jude 1-2

Be all the more eager to make your calling and election sure. For if you do these things, you will never fall, and you will receive a rich welcome into the eternal kingdom of our Lord and Savior Jesus Christ.

2 Peter 1:10-11

Do not repay evil with evil or insult with insult, but with blessing, because to this you were called so that you may inherit a blessing.

1 Peter 3:9

Live a life worthy of the calling you have received.

Ephesians 4:1

The LORD came and stood there, calling as at the other times, "Samuel! Samuel!" Then Samuel said, "Speak, for your servant is listening."

1 Samuel 3:10

GOD'S CALL

Every year, thousands of young adults await "the call." They sit eagerly by the phone, hoping that it will ring and that on the other end will be someone with the best news (humanly speaking) they will ever hear.

"Hello, Beth? I'm calling from the Phoenix Mercury. We just wanted you to know that we've selected you in the second round. We're looking forward to having you on our team."

Whether it's a call from the WNBA, major league baseball, the NBA or the NFL, "the call" is the thrill of a lifetime.

It means the culmination of a dream and the beginning of an incredible adventure.

But it cannot compare with the kind of call Samuel got when he was a youngster serving in Eli's home.

"Samuel!" called a voice. The boy, thinking Eli had summoned him, ran to his master.

Eventually, Eli realized that the voice was God's. He told Samuel to listen and heed God's voice.

Samuel listened as God foretold some really bad news for Eli and Eli's family. It would be the beginning of Samuel's own grand adventure as he became God's trusted prophet.

"The call" changed everything for Samuel. And God is calling us as well. He is urging us to follow him. He is calling us to serve him, glorify him and spread the Good News about him.

GOD'S CONTROL OF THE ACTION

God said, "Let there be light," and there was light.

Genesis 1:3

"As the rain and the snow
  come down from heaven,
and do not return to it
  without watering the earth
and making it bud and flourish, ...
so is my word that goes out from my mouth:
  It will not return to me empty,
but will accomplish what I desire
  and achieve the purpose for which I sent it,"
    declares the LORD.

Isaiah 55:10-11

God determines the number of the stars
  and calls them each by name.
Great is our Lord and mighty in power;
  his understanding has no limit.

Psalm 147:4-5

Since the creation of the world God's invisible qualities—his eternal power and divine nature—have been clearly seen, being understood from what has been made.

Romans 1:20

GOD'S CONTROL
OF THE ACTION

God is the King of all the earth;
   sing to him a psalm of praise.
God reigns over the nations;
   God is seated on his holy throne.

Psalm 47:7-8

To him who is able to do immeasurably more than all we ask or imagine, according to his power that is at work within us, to him be glory in the church and in Christ Jesus throughout all generations, for ever and ever! Amen.

Ephesians 3:20-21

The plans of the LORD stand firm forever,
   the purposes of his heart through all genera-tions.

Psalm 33:11

O LORD, God of our fathers, are you not the God who is in heaven? You rule over all the kingdoms of the nations. Power and might are in your hand, and no one can withstand you.

2 Chronicles 20:6

Many are the plans in a man's heart,
   but it is the LORD's purpose that prevails.

Proverbs 19:21

GOD'S CONTROL
OF THE ACTION

Yours, O LORD, is the kingdom;
    you are exalted as head over all.
Wealth and honor come from you;
    you are the ruler of all things.

1 Chronicles 29:11-12

The LORD has established his throne in heaven,
    and his kingdom rules over all.

Psalm 103:19

You are the God who performs miracles;
    you display your power among the peoples.

Psalm 77:14

The Sovereign LORD comes with power,
    and his arm rules for him.

Isaiah 40:10

Hallelujah!
    For our Lord God Almighty reigns.
Let us rejoice and be glad
    and give him glory!

Revelation 19:6-7

GOD'S CONTROL
OF THE ACTION

As the book of Esther was being written, a funny thing happened: The name of God was not mentioned. Esther is the only book in the Bible in which God's holy name does not appear.

Early in the 2000-2001 college basketball season, the coach of the University of Wisconsin, Dick Bennett, retired. The season had already started, and the team had played several games. But Bennett, a Christian, decided that it was time to give up coaching. He had become something of a legend in Wisconsin, and he was successful, but he decided to call it a career.

For the next eight games, Wisconsin was unbeatable. Led by Brad Soderberg, the new coach, they continued to win. And much of the credit went to Bennett. He wasn't there. He didn't run practices. He was no longer on the bench shouting instructions. Most of the time, his name wasn't even mentioned. But his influence was still there.

In a much more specific way, God influenced the situation in the book of Esther without even being mentioned. Unlike Bennett, this wasn't a case of an extension of a philosophy; God actually interceded for Esther and her people.

God is the often-unacknowledged controller of the universe and the unnamed provider of our every need. God's works shout his presence, even when his name is not mentioned.

GOD'S GAME PLAN

"I know the plans I have for you," declares the LORD, "plans to prosper you and not to harm you, plans to give you hope and a future."

Jeremiah 29:11

Be joyful always; pray continually; give thanks in all circumstances, for this is God's will for you in Christ Jesus.

1 Thessalonians 5:16-18

Praise be to the God and Father of our Lord Jesus Christ, who has blessed us in the heavenly realms with every spiritual blessing in Christ. For he chose us in him before the creation of the world to be holy and blameless in his sight. In love he predestined us to be adopted as his sons through Jesus Christ, in accordance with his pleasure and will-to the praise of his glorious grace, which he has freely given us in the One he loves.

Ephesians 1:3-6

It is God's will that you should be sanctified.

1 Thessalonians 4:3

Just as he who called you is holy, so be holy in all you do; for it is written: "Be holy, because I am holy."

1 Peter 1:15-16

GOD'S GAME PLAN

Those God foreknew he also predestined to be conformed to the likeness of his Son, that he might be the firstborn among many brothers. And those he predestined, he also called; those he called, he also justified; those he justified, he also glorified.

Romans 8:29-30

Do not conform any longer to the pattern of this world, but be transformed by the renewing of your mind. Then you will be able to test and approve what God's will is—his good, pleasing and perfect will.

Romans 12:2

Live holy and godly lives as you look forward to the day of God and speed its coming.

2 Peter 3:11-12

We know that when Christ appears, we shall be like him, for we shall see him as he is. Everyone who has this hope in him purifies himself, just as he is pure.

1 John 3:2-3

Surely you desire truth in the inner parts, O LORD;
you teach me wisdom in the inmost place.

Psalm 51:6

GOD'S GAME PLAN

I desire to do your will, O my God;
   your law is within my heart.

Psalm 40:8

*We have not stopped praying for you and asking
God to fill you with the knowledge of his will
through all spiritual wisdom and understanding.
And we pray this in order that you may live a life
worthy of the Lord and may please him in every
way: bearing fruit in every good work, growing in
the knowledge of God, being strengthened with all
power according to his glorious might so that you
may have great endurance and patience, and joy-
fully giving thanks to the Father, who has qualified
you to share in the inheritance of the saints in the
kingdom of light.*

Colossians 1:9-12

*May the God of peace, who through the blood of
the eternal covenant brought back from the dead
our Lord Jesus, that great Shepherd of the sheep,
equip you with everything good for doing his will,
and may he work in us what is pleasing to him,
through Jesus Christ, to whom be glory for ever
and ever. Amen.*

Hebrews 13:20-21

Devotional Thought on

GOD'S GAME PLAN

As a high school basketball coach, I never went into a practice without a written plan.

Through the years, as my own children worked their way through a series of coaches at different levels, I saw some coaches who didn't see eye to eye with me and my approach. They didn't have a plan, and their practices were chaotic. Often they appeared to be overseeing recess, as each athlete did whatever he or she pleased.

This is what it was like during the days of the judges, a time when "everyone did as he saw fit" (Judges 17:6). But it wasn't God's fault. He had clearly laid out the guidelines the people should have been using. He gave them the law. He gave them the covenants. They knew what was what.

Sometimes my players would depart from my design. I would have to call a time out and "gently" suggest that they return to doing it my way. God had to do that with Israel on several occasions.

For us, we have a clear and unmistakable game plan. Our goal is to work together with other believers to glorify God, to live in a way that pleases him and to spread the gospel. We need to stick to God's plan or we'll look like an eighth-grade basketball team that doesn't have a prayer.

GOD'S OFFICIATING

The LORD reigns forever;
    he has established his throne for judgment.
He will judge the world in righteousness;
    he will govern the peoples with justice.

Psalm 9:7-8

*The word of God is living and active. Sharper than
any double-edged sword, it penetrates even to
dividing soul and spirit, joints and marrow; it
judges the thoughts and attitudes of the heart.
Nothing in all creation is hidden from God's sight.
Everything is uncovered and laid bare before the
eyes of him to whom we must give account.*

Hebrews 4:12-13

The LORD is known by his justice.

Psalm 9:16

Against you, you only, O LORD, have I sinned
    and done what is evil in your sight,
so that you are proved right when you speak
    and justified when you judge....
Cleanse me with hyssop, and I will be clean;
    wash me, and I will be whiter than snow.

Psalm 51:4, 7

GOD'S OFFICIATING

The LORD loves righteousness and justice;
the earth is full of his unfailing love.

Psalm 33:5

It is the Lord who judges me.

1 Corinthians 4:4

Righteousness and justice are the foundation of
your throne;
love and faithfulness go before you.
Blessed are those who have learned to acclaim
you,
who walk in the light of your presence, O LORD.

Psalm 89:14-15

Surely there is a God who judges the earth.

Psalm 58:11

The LORD, the LORD, the compassionate and
gracious God, slow to anger, abounding in love
and faithfulness, maintaining love to thousands,
and forgiving wickedness, rebellion and sin.
Yet he does not leave the guilty unpunished.

Exodus 34:6-7

"I am the LORD, who exercises kindness,
justice and righteousness on earth,
for in these I delight."

Jeremiah 9:24

GOD'S OFFICIATING

The LORD will judge the ends of the earth.

1 Samuel 2:10

Let the heavens rejoice, let the earth be glad;
   let them say among the nations, "The LORD
reigns!"
Let the sea resound, and all that is in it;
   let the fields be jubilant, and everything in them!
Then the trees of the forest will sing,
   they will sing for joy before the LORD,
   for he comes to judge the earth.

1 Chronicles 16:31-33

Will not the Judge of all the earth do right?

Genesis 18:25

The LORD will judge the world in righteousness
   and the peoples in his truth.

Psalm 96:13

God is a righteous judge.

Psalm 7:11

GOD'S OFFICIATING

The law will go out from Zion,
   the word of the LORD from Jerusalem.
He will judge between the nations
   and will settle disputes for many peoples.

Isaiah 2:3-4

The LORD takes his place in court;
   he rises to judge the people.

Isaiah 3:13

The Spirit of the LORD will rest on Jesus—
   the Spirit of wisdom and of understanding,
   the Spirit of counsel and of power,
   the Spirit of knowledge and of the fear of the
LORD —
and he will delight in the fear of the LORD.

He will not judge by what he sees with his eyes,
   or decide by what he hears with his ears;
but with righteousness he will judge the needy,
   with justice he will give decisions for the
poor of the earth.

Isaiah 11:2-4

GOD'S OFFICIATING

We will all stand before God's judgment seat.

Romans 14:10

The LORD is compassionate and gracious,
   slow to anger, abounding in love....
He does not treat us as our sins deserve
   or repay us according to our iniquities.

Psalm 103:8, 10

*All have sinned and fall short of the glory of God,
and are justified freely by his grace through the
redemption that came by Christ Jesus. God presented him as a sacrifice of atonement, through
faith in his blood. He did this to demonstrate his
justice, because in his forbearance he had left the
sins committed beforehand unpunished—he did it
to demonstrate his justice at the present time, so as
to be just and the one who justifies those who
have faith in Jesus.*

Romans 3:23-26

*I have fought the good fight, I have finished the
race, I have kept the faith. Now there is in store for
me the crown of righteousness, which the Lord,
the righteous Judge, will award to me on that
day—and not only to me, but also to all who have
longed for his appearing.*

2 Timothy 4:7-8

GOD'S OFFICIATING

We may sit in the high school bleachers and decide that the basketball referee may as well not even be looking at the game. But in reality we know that is not the way things work with basketball officials. Referees have to make impartial calls based on the facts as they see them—not based on the fact that their nephew plays for one of the teams or for some other sentimental reason.

While referees may strive for impartiality, they can never be as completely impartial as our heavenly Father. Peter said this about God's ability to judge with clarity: "Since you call on a Father who judges each man's work impartially, live your lives as strangers here in reverent fear" (1 Peter 1:17). God is absolutely just, and he considers each person's situation fairly.

This is one of the reasons we can trust him. He judges from a heart that has compassion for us, yet he does so from a perspective that demands justice. And because of who he is, he is perfect in all his judgments.

Therefore, it is up to us to live "in reverent fear," realizing how vital it is that we maintain an unwavering faith in God. He rules and reigns with both his eyes and his heart, and he rules correctly 100 percent of the time.

GOD'S TEAM

Jesus said, "On this rock I will build my church, and the gates of Hades will not overcome it."

Matthew 16:18

God has said: "I will live with them and walk among them, and I will be their God, and they will be my people."

2 Corinthians 6:16

Come, let us bow down in worship,
 let us kneel before the LORD our Maker;
for he is our God
 and we are the people of his pasture,
 the flock under his care.

Psalm 95:6-7

How great is the love the Father has lavished on us, that we should be called children of God! And that is what we are!

1 John 3:1

Both the one who makes men holy and those who are made holy are of the same family. So Jesus is not ashamed to call them brothers.

Hebrews 2:11

GOD'S TEAM

You are no longer foreigners and aliens, but fellow citizens with God's people and members of God's household, built on the foundation of the apostles and prophets, with Christ Jesus himself as the chief cornerstone. In him the whole building is joined together and rises to become a holy temple in the Lord. And in him you too are being built together to become a dwelling in which God lives by his Spirit.

Ephesians 2:19-22

You are all sons of God through faith in Christ Jesus, for all of you who were baptized into Christ have clothed yourselves with Christ. There is neither Jew nor Greek, slave nor free, male nor female, for you are all one in Christ Jesus.

Galatians 3:26-28

I kneel before the Father, from whom his whole family in heaven and on earth derives its name. I pray that out of his glorious riches he may strengthen you with power through his Spirit in your inner being, so that Christ may dwell in your hearts through faith.

Ephesians 3:14-17

GOD'S TEAM

The disciples were called Christians first at Antioch.

Acts 11:26

God placed all things under Jesus' feet and appointed him to be head over everything for the church, which is his body, the fullness of him who fills everything in every way.

Ephesians 1:22-23

Christ is the head of the church, his body, of which he is the Savior.

Ephesians 5:23

I am writing you these instructions so that, if I am delayed, you will know how people ought to conduct themselves in God's household, which is the church of the living God, the pillar and foundation of the truth.

1 Timothy 3:14-15

You have come to Mount Zion, to the heavenly Jerusalem, the city of the living God. You have come to thousands upon thousands of angels in joyful assembly, to the church of the firstborn, whose names are written in heaven. You have come to God, the judge of all men, to the spirits of righteous men made perfect, to Jesus the mediator of a new covenant.

Hebrews 12:22-24

GOD'S TEAM

Through the gospel the Gentiles are heirs together with Israel, members together of one body, and sharers together in the promise in Christ Jesus.

Ephesians 3:6

Consider Abraham: "He believed God, and it was credited to him as righteousness." Understand, then, that those who believe are children of Abraham. The Scripture foresaw that God would justify the Gentiles by faith, and announced the gospel in advance to Abraham: "All nations will be blessed through you." So those who have faith are blessed along with Abraham, the man of faith.

Galatians 3:6-9

God sent his Son, born of a woman, born under law, to redeem those under law, that we might receive the full rights of sons. Because you are sons, God sent the Spirit of his Son into our hearts, the Spirit who calls out, "Abba, Father." So you are no longer a slave, but a son; and since you are a son, God has made you also an heir.

Galatians 4:4-7

GOD'S TEAM

Those who are led by the Spirit of God are sons of God. For you did not receive a spirit that makes you a slave again to fear, but you received the Spirit of sonship. And by him we cry, "Abba, Father." The Spirit himself testifies with our spirit that we are God's children. Now if we are children, then we are heirs-heirs of God and co-heirs with Christ, if indeed we share in his sufferings in order that we may also share in his glory.

Romans 8:14-17

Remember that formerly you who are Gentiles by birth ... were separate from Christ, excluded from citizenship in Israel and foreigners to the covenants of the promise, without hope and without God in the world. But now in Christ Jesus you who once were far away have been brought near through the blood of Christ.

Ephesians 2:11-13

Now you are the body of Christ, and each one of you is a part of it.

1 Corinthians 12:27

You are a chosen people, a royal priesthood, a holy nation, a people belonging to God, that you may declare the praises of him who called you out of darkness into his wonderful light. Once you were not a people, but now you are the people of God.

1 Peter 2:9-10

GOD'S TEAM

When I first coached varsity basketball, our high school was new and had previously fielded just one varsity team. There was no tradition, no history and hardly any uniforms. That's why I felt it was important to do all I could to build the team into something the school could take pride in.

Peter wrote this letter (1 Peter) at time when the church was beginning a new era. But Peter wanted the people of the church to know who they were. What he said about the Christians in the early church (1 Peter 2:9-10) is still valid today. We as believers in Jesus Christ are:

- a chosen people—what once applied only to the Jews now applies to believers of both Jewish and Gentile heritage;

- a royal priesthood—each individual believer in Jesus is a priest, able to communicate directly with God;

- a holy nation—God wants each believer to strive for holiness; and

- a people belonging to God—as Christians, we are possessors of the new covenant (the new thing God is working through those who trust Jesus Christ).

What a team! Like my old basketball squad, we are united in our purpose and spurred on by our mission.

GOD'S WATCHFULNESS

The eyes of the LORD are on those who fear him,
  on those whose hope is in his unfailing love.

Psalm 33:18

God will not let your foot slip—
  he who watches over you will not slumber;
indeed, he who watches over Israel
  will neither slumber nor sleep.

Psalm 121:3-4

*This is what the Sovereign LORD says: I myself will
search for my sheep and look after them. As a
shepherd looks after his scattered flock when he is
with them, so will I look after my sheep.*

Ezekiel 34:11-12

Where can I go from your Spirit?
  Where can I flee from your presence?
If I go up to the heavens, you are there;
  if I make my bed in the depths, you are there.
If I rise on the wings of the dawn,
  if I settle on the far side of the sea,
even there your hand will guide me,
  your right hand will hold me fast.

Psalm 139:7-10

GOD'S WATCHFULNESS

The eyes of the LORD are on the righteous
and his ears are attentive to their cry.

Psalm 34:15

Unless the LORD watches over the city,
the watchmen stand guard in vain.

Psalm 127:1

God tends his flock like a shepherd:
He gathers the lambs in his arms
and carries them close to his heart;
he gently leads those that have young.

Isaiah 40:11

The LORD watches over all who love him.

Psalm 145:20

God shielded him and cared for him;
he guarded him as the apple of his eye.

Deuteronomy 32:10

GOD'S WATCHFULNESS

The LORD will keep you from all harm—
   he will watch over your life;
the LORD will watch over your coming and going
   both now and forevermore.

Psalm 121:7-8

The Lord watches over the way of the righteous.

Psalm 1:6

The LORD bless you
   and keep you;
the LORD make his face shine upon you
   and be gracious to you;
the LORD turn his face toward you
   and give you peace.

Numbers 6:24-26

He who scattered Israel will gather them
   and will watch over his flock like a shepherd.

Jeremiah 31:10

GOD'S
WATCHFULNESS

The most remarkable assembly of basketball talent took place in the late 1990s when the National Basketball Association brought together the 50 greatest players of all time. One by one they assembled on the court.

Reunions are sometimes mammoth projects. They involve moving people and accommodating people.

But no reunion anyone has ever planned can compare with the one Ezekiel talked about in Ezekiel 11. "This is what the Sovereign LORD says: I will gather you from the nations and bring you back from the countries where you have been scattered, and I will give you back the land of Israel again" (Ezekiel 11:17). And God did.

He sheltered his people in the land of their exile (see Ezekiel 11:16), and later the leaders of the countries to which his people had been scattered would be led by God to let the people freely go.

A person may move hundreds of miles away into a land that is foreign—yet all the while God is watching over that person and preparing for the day that person will return home. Even during the exile of his chosen people, there was never a moment when God took his eyes off them or let them depart from his heart. That's the only way that this reunion of such great proportions could be carried out.

GOD'S WISDOM

"My thoughts are not your thoughts,
neither are your ways my ways,"
declares the LORD.
"As the heavens are higher than the earth,
so are my ways higher than your ways
and my thoughts than your thoughts."

Isaiah 55:8-9

Can anyone teach knowledge to God,
since he judges even the highest?

Job 21:22

God made the earth by his power;
he founded the world by his wisdom
and stretched out the heavens by his understanding.

Jeremiah 10:12

Praise be to the name of God for ever and ever;
wisdom and power are his.

Daniel 2:20

GOD'S WISDOM

By wisdom the LORD laid the earth's foundations,
  by understanding he set the heavens in place;
by his knowledge the deeps were divided,
  and the clouds let drop the dew.

Proverbs 3:19-20

The LORD Almighty,
  wonderful in counsel and magnificent in
wisdom.

Isaiah 28:29

To God belong wisdom and power;
  counsel and understanding are his.

Job 12:13

Who has understood the mind of the LORD,
  or instructed him as his counselor?
Whom did the LORD consult to enlighten him,
  and who taught him the right way?
Who was it that taught him knowledge
  or showed him the path of understanding?

Isaiah 40:13-14

GOD'S WISDOM

How many are your works, O LORD!
   In wisdom you made them all;
   the earth is full of your creatures.

Psalm 104:24

You alone are the LORD. You made the heavens,
even the highest heavens, and all their starry host,
the earth and all that is on it, the seas and all that is
in them. You give life to everything, and the multi-
tudes of heaven worship you.

Nehemiah 9:6

"To whom will you compare me?
   Or who is my equal?" says the Holy One.
Lift your eyes and look to the heavens:
   Who created all these?
He who brings out the starry host one by one,
   and calls them each by name.

Isaiah 40:25-26

To the only wise God be glory forever through
Jesus Christ!

Romans 16:27

GOD'S WISDOM

In Christ we have redemption through his blood, the forgiveness of sins, in accordance with the riches of God's grace that he lavished on us with all wisdom and understanding.

Ephesians 1:7-8

We speak of God's secret wisdom, a wisdom that has been hidden and that God destined for our glory before time began.

1 Corinthians 2:7

We have not received the spirit of the world but the Spirit who is from God, that we may understand what God has freely given us. This is what we speak, not in words taught us by human wisdom but in words taught by the Spirit, expressing spiritual truths in spiritual words. The man without the Spirit does not accept the things that come from the Spirit of God, for they are foolishness to him, and he cannot understand them, because they are spiritually discerned. The spiritual man makes judgments about all things, but he himself is not subject to any man's judgment:

"For who has known the mind of the Lord that he may instruct him?"

But we have the mind of Christ.

1 Corinthians 2:12-16

GOD'S WISDOM

The foolishness of God is wiser than man's wisdom, and the weakness of God is stronger than man's strength.

1 Corinthians 1:25

O LORD, you have searched me
and you know me.
You know when I sit and when I rise;
you perceive my thoughts from afar.
You discern my going out and my lying down;
you are familiar with all my ways.
Before a word is on my tongue
you know it completely, O LORD.

You hem me in—behind and before;
you have laid your hand upon me.
Such knowledge is too wonderful for me,
too lofty for me to attain.

Psalm 139:1-6

Oh, the depth of the riches of the wisdom and knowledge of God!
How unsearchable his judgments,
and his paths beyond tracing out!

Romans 11:33

GOD'S WISDOM

Although I was a high school basketball coach for five years, I cannot even begin to think I understand the intricacies of coaching as do people like Mike Krzyzewski and Tom Izzo. Those two expert coaches, along with the many other coaches who have spent their careers analyzing basketball, have knowledge of, and insight into, the game that I will never have.

For those of us who follow these kinds of coaches, there is no shame in admitting that we cannot know their ways and thoughts. And we are not wrong to marvel at their skills as coaches. We would be foolish to second-guess them and assume that we know what would work better than they do.

Now let's move that thinking up a couple of million notches. Let's think about God and us. God knows so very much more than we could ever even hope to know. He has the wisdom of omniscience and the power of omnipotence at his disposal—and it is our privilege to call him our God.

Just as there is no shame in admitting that Mike Krzyzewski knows more about basketball than I do, there is no shame in acquiescing to the greatness of God. His way is the way of majesty and splendor. Let's enjoy him for who he is.

GODLINESS

Jesus said, "A student is not above his teacher, but everyone who is fully trained will be like his teacher."

Luke 6:40

Godliness with contentment is great gain.

1 Timothy 6:6

Make every effort to add to your faith goodness; and to goodness, knowledge; and to knowledge, self-control; and to self-control, perseverance; and to perseverance, godliness; and to godliness, brotherly kindness; and to brotherly kindness, love.

2 Peter 1:5-7

You were taught, with regard to your former way of life, to put off your old self, which is being corrupted by its deceitful desires; to be made new in the attitude of your minds; and to put on the new self, created to be like God in true righteousness and holiness.

Ephesians 4:22-24

You were once darkness, but now you are light in the Lord. Live as children of light (for the fruit of the light consists in all goodness, righteousness and truth) and find out what pleases the Lord.

Ephesians 5:8-10

GODLINESS

Be imitators of God, therefore, as dearly loved children and live a life of love, just as Christ loved us and gave himself up for us as a fragrant offering and sacrifice to God.

Ephesians 5:1-2

Paul, a servant of God and an apostle of Jesus Christ for the faith of God's elect and the knowledge of the truth that leads to godliness—a faith and knowledge resting on the hope of eternal life, which God, who does not lie, promised before the beginning of time.

Titus 1:1-2

Be kind and compassionate to one another, forgiving each other, just as in Christ God forgave you.

Ephesians 4:32

This is how we know what love is: Jesus Christ laid down his life for us. And we ought to lay down our lives for our brothers.

1 John 3:16

Train yourself to be godly. For physical training is of some value, but godliness has value for all things, holding promise for both the present life and the life to come.

1 Timothy 4:7-8

GODLINESS

The LORD has dealt with me according to my
righteousness;
    according to the cleanness of my hands he
has rewarded me.
For I have kept the ways of the LORD;
    I have not done evil by turning from my God.
All his laws are before me;
    I have not turned away from his decrees.
I have been blameless before him
    and have kept myself from sin.
The LORD has rewarded me according to my
righteousness,
    according to my cleanness in his sight.

2 Samuel 22:21-25

As long as I have life within me,
    the breath of God in my nostrils,
my lips will not speak wickedness,
    and my tongue will utter no deceit....
I will maintain my righteousness and never let
go of it;
    my conscience will not reproach me as long
as I live.

Job 27:3-4, 6

Lead me, O LORD, in your righteousness ...
    make straight your way before me.

Psalm 5:8

GODLINESS

To the faithful, O Lord, you show yourself faithful,
    to the blameless you show yourself blameless,
to the pure you show yourself pure.

2 Samuel 22:26-27

Commit your way to the Lord;
    trust in him and he will do this:
He will make your righteousness shine like the
dawn,
    the justice of your cause like the noonday sun.

Psalm 37:5-6

From everlasting to everlasting
    the Lord's love is with those who fear him,
    and his righteousness with their children's
children—
with those who keep his covenant
    and remember to obey his precepts.

Psalm 103:17-18

The righteousness of the blameless makes a
straight way for them.

Proverbs 11:5

GODLINESS

Let us love one another, for love comes from God. Everyone who loves has been born of God and knows God. Whoever does not love does not know God, because God is love. This is how God showed his love among us: He sent his one and only Son into the world that we might live through him. This is love: not that we loved God, but that he loved us and sent his Son as an atoning sacrifice for our sins. Dear friends, since God so loved us, we also ought to love one another.

1 John 4:7-11

The grace of God that brings salvation has appeared to all men. It teaches us to say "No" to ungodliness and worldly passions, and to live self-controlled, upright and godly lives in this present age, while we wait for the blessed hope—the glorious appearing of our great God and Savior, Jesus Christ, who gave himself for us to redeem us from all wickedness and to purify for himself a people that are his very own, eager to do what is good.

Titus 2:11-14

God's divine power has given us everything we need for life and godliness through our knowledge of him who called us by his own glory and goodness.

2 Peter 1:3

GODLINESS

Perhaps the athlete who has been the hero to the most people was Michael Jordan. He became the ultimate mirrored image. His commercial that gave us the phrase "I want to be like Mike" set the tone, and fans ate it up. Millions wanted to be like Mike because of his charisma, his style and his incomparable basketball skills.

But did you ever think about wanting to be like Micah?

There's a good reason for choosing Micah as a person to emulate, and it has nothing to do with hitting long-range jump shots to clinch NBA titles. No, it's because the prophet Micah's name, excitingly enough, means "Who is like the LORD?" The answer to this question is that no one is like our God. He alone is holy and good.

But maybe we can strive to be a little more like God every day and so become closer to him. Maybe if we learned to live like Micah, to trust God to transform our hearts and our character as we live in obedience to his truth in our everyday lives, we'll become more like the God we long to serve.

Do we want to be like Micah? If it means having a new appreciation for God's holiness and greatness, then we should go for it!

GOOD JUDGMENT

Preserve sound judgment and discernment,
   do not let them out of your sight;
they will be life for you,
   an ornament to grace your neck.
Then you will go on your way in safety,
   and your foot will not stumble;
when you lie down, you will not be afraid;
   when you lie down, your sleep will be sweet.

Proverbs 3:21-24

God gives wisdom to the wise
   and knowledge to the discerning.
He reveals deep and hidden things;
   he knows what lies in darkness,
   and light dwells with him.

Daniel 2:21-22

Do good to your servant
   according to your word, O LORD.
Teach me knowledge and good judgment,
   for I believe in your commands.

Psalm 119:65-66

The heart of the discerning acquires knowledge;
   the ears of the wise seek it out.

Proverbs 18:15

GOOD JUDGMENT

Wisdom reposes in the heart of the discerning.

Proverbs 14:33

Wisdom has built her house;
    she has hewn out its seven pillars.
She has prepared her meat and mixed her wine;
    she has also set her table.
She has sent out her maids, and she calls
    from the highest point of the city.
"Let all who are simple come in here!"
    she says to those who lack judgment.
"Come, eat my food
    and drink the wine I have mixed.
Leave your simple ways and you will live;
    walk in the way of understanding."

Proverbs 9:1-6

May the LORD give you discretion and understanding.

1 Chronicles 22:12

A discerning man keeps wisdom in view.

Proverbs 17:24

Those who are wise will shine like the brightness of the heavens.

Daniel 12:3

GOOD JUDGMENT

Teach us to number our days aright, O LORD,
that we may gain a heart of wisdom.

Psalm 90:12

*Do not accept a bribe, for a bribe blinds the eyes
of the wise and twists the words of the righteous.
Follow justice and justice alone, so that you may
live and possess the land the LORD your God is giving you.*

Deuteronomy 16:19-20

*King Solomon was greater in riches and wisdom
than all the other kings of the earth. The whole
world sought audience with Solomon to hear the
wisdom God had put in his heart.*

1 Kings 10:23-24

The law of the LORD is perfect,
reviving the soul.
The statutes of the LORD are trustworthy,
making wise the simple.
The precepts of the LORD are right,
giving joy to the heart.
The commands of the LORD are radiant,
giving light to the eyes.

Psalms 19:7-8

GOOD JUDGMENT

A man's wisdom gives him patience.

Proverbs 19:11

The mouth of the righteous man utters wisdom,
    and his tongue speaks what is just.
The law of his God is in his heart;
    his feet do not slip.

Psalm 37:30-31

Blessed is the man who finds wisdom,
    the man who gains understanding,
for she is more profitable than silver
    and yields better returns than gold.
She is more precious than rubies;
    nothing you desire can compare with her.
Long life is in her right hand;
    in her left hand are riches and honor.
Her ways are pleasant ways,
    and all her paths are peace.
She is a tree of life to those who embrace her;
    those who lay hold of her will be blessed.

Proverbs 3:13-18

GOOD JUDGMENT

My son, if you accept my words
    and store up my commands within you,
turning your ear to wisdom
    and applying your heart to understanding,
and if you call out for insight
    and cry aloud for understanding,
and if you look for it as for silver
    and search for it as for hidden treasure,
then you will understand the fear of the LORD
    and find the knowledge of God.
For the LORD gives wisdom,
    and from his mouth come knowledge and
understanding.
He holds victory in store for the upright,
    he is a shield to those whose walk is blameless,
for he guards the course of the just
    and protects the way of his faithful ones.

Then you will understand what is right and just
    and fair—every good path.
For wisdom will enter your heart,
    and knowledge will be pleasant to your soul.
Discretion will protect you,
    and understanding will guard you.

Proverbs 2:1-11

GOOD JUDGMENT

Remember this old saying you might have heard your parents repeat: "Nothing good ever happens after midnight"? That should be put on a plaque and hung on the wall of every locker room in the country.

Far too often, we hear of athletes who are in the wrong place at the wrong time—putting their careers in jeopardy because of it.

The book of Proverbs suggests that a person who lives by wisdom's guidance will be saved from the "ways of wicked men" (Proverbs 2:12).

Funny thing is, it's not hard to discern who "wicked men" are. In fact, some leagues have special seminars for rookies to help them learn what types of people and situations to avoid.

If the new players need some help, we can suggest Proverbs 2:12-14 to them. Here are the kinds of people one should avoid:

1. Those "whose words are perverse"

2. Those who "leave the straight paths to walk in dark ways"

3. Those who "delight in doing wrong"

The next time you read about an athlete who stumbled into trouble, remind yourself of these verses. It is vital that you steer clear of those who might lead you in a direction that neither you nor God wants you to take.

HECKLERS

The LORD mocks proud mockers
but gives grace to the humble.

Proverbs 3:34

I will exalt you, O LORD,
for you lifted me out of the depths
and did not let my enemies gloat over me.

Psalm 30:1

Have mercy on us, O LORD, have mercy on us,
for we have endured much contempt.
We have endured much ridicule from the proud,
much contempt from the arrogant.

Psalm 123:3-4

O my Strength, I watch for you;
you, O God, are my fortress, my loving God.

God will go before me
and will let me gloat over those who slander me.

Psalm 59:9-10

HECKLERS

You are a shield around me, O LORD;
  you bestow glory on me and lift up my head.
To the LORD I cry aloud,
  and he answers me from his holy hill.

Psalm 3:3-4

Do not gloat over me, my enemy!
  Though I have fallen, I will rise.
Though I sit in darkness,
  the LORD will be my light.

Micah 7:8

Remove from me scorn and contempt, O LORD,
  for I keep your statutes.
Though rulers sit together and slander me,
  your servant will meditate on your decrees.
Your statutes are my delight;
  they are my counselors.

Psalm 119:22-24

The humble will rejoice in the LORD;
  the needy will rejoice in the Holy One of Israel.
The ruthless will vanish,
  the mockers will disappear.

Isaiah 29:19-20

HECKLERS

For your name's sake, O LORD, preserve my life;
    in your righteousness, bring me out of trouble.
In your unfailing love, silence my enemies …
    for I am your servant.

Psalm 143:11-12

To you, O LORD, I lift up my soul;
    in you I trust, O my God.
Do not let me be put to shame,
    nor let my enemies triumph over me.
No one whose hope is in you
    will ever be put to shame.

Psalm 25:1-3

Awake, and rise to my defense!
    Contend for me, my God and Lord.
Vindicate me in your righteousness, O LORD my God;
    do not let them gloat over me.

Psalm 35:23-24

Though I walk in the midst of trouble, O LORD,
    you preserve my life;
you stretch out your hand against the anger of my foes,
    with your right hand you save me.

Psalm 138:7

HECKLERS

As a high school athlete, I loved being out on the court or the field playing basketball or baseball. But when the games or practices were over, I didn't particularly enjoy what was next.

The locker room.

Often the locker room is not a very nice place for a young Christian athlete to be. The talk is often dirty; the subjects are often embarrassing, and the goings-on are often rude and distasteful.

When you're the lone Christian in the middle of all this, it's easy to feel a little like David felt in Psalm 35. He was around people who slandered him mercilessly. They mocked him, said untrue things about him.

But David stayed true to God. He continued to trust that God would do what was right in regard to those ruthless people. And David continued to speak of God's righteousness while continually praising him.

Whether we face it in the locker room or on the job or even in the family, it's not easy to be mocked because of what we stand for. But we should not try to withstand these types of situations without God's help. David said to God, "Do not be far from me, O LORD" (Psalm 35:22). When mockers arise, we need to stay focused on God's eagerness to assist us at all times and under all conditions.

IDOLS

*"I am the L*ORD* your God....*
You shall have no other gods before me.
You shall not make for yourself an idol in the form
of anything in heaven above or on the earth
beneath or in the waters below."

Exodus 20:2-4

"I am the LORD; that is my name!
  I will not give my glory to another
  or my praise to idols."

Isaiah 42:8

Since ... you have been raised with Christ, set your
hearts on things above, where Christ is seated at
the right hand of God. Set your minds on things
above, not on earthly things. For you died, and
your life is now hidden with Christ in God. When
Christ, who is your life, appears, then you also will
appear with him in glory.

Colossians 3:1-4

Those who cling to worthless idols
  forfeit the grace that could be theirs.
But I, with a song of thanksgiving,
  will sacrifice to you, O LORD.

Jonah 2:8-9

IDOLS

Serve the LORD with all your heart. Do not turn away after useless idols. They can do you no good, nor can they rescue you, because they are useless.

1 Samuel 12:20-21

Jesus said, "Do not store up for yourselves treasures on earth, where moth and rust destroy, and where thieves break in and steal. But store up for yourselves treasures in heaven, where moth and rust do not destroy, and where thieves do not break in and steal. For where your treasure is, there your heart will be also."

Matthew 6:19-21

We fix our eyes not on what is seen, but on what is unseen. For what is seen is temporary, but what is unseen is eternal.

2 Corinthians 4:18

Do not love the world or anything in the world. If anyone loves the world, the love of the Father is not in him. For everything in the world—the cravings of sinful man, the lust of his eyes and the boasting of what he has and does—comes not from the Father but from the world.

1 John 2:15-16

IDOLS

Even while these people were worshiping the LORD, they were serving their idols.

2 Kings 17:41

"My people have exchanged their Glory
   for worthless idols,"
      declares the LORD.

Jeremiah 2:11

They followed worthless idols and themselves became worthless.

2 Kings 17:15

They exchanged the truth of God for a lie, and worshiped and served created things rather than the Creator—who is forever praised.

Romans 1:25

Do not turn to idols.

Leviticus 19:4

Who may ascend the hill of the LORD?
   Who may stand in his holy place?
He who has clean hands and a pure heart,
   who does not lift up his soul to an idol
   or swear by what is false.
He will receive blessing from the LORD
   and vindication from God his Savior.

Psalm 24:3-5

IDOLS

Do any of the worthless idols of the nations
bring rain?
    Do the skies themselves send down showers?
No, it is you, O LORD our God.
    Therefore our hope is in you,
    for you are the one who does all this.

Jeremiah 14:22

Do men make their own gods?
    Yes, but they are not gods!

Jeremiah 16:20

*No immoral, impure or greedy person—such a
man is an idolater—has any inheritance in the
kingdom of Christ and of God.*

Ephesians 5:5

*This is what the Sovereign LORD says: Repent! Turn
from your idols.*

Ezekiel 14:6

My dear friends, flee from idolatry.

1 Corinthians 10:14

*You turned to God from idols to serve the living
and true God.*

1 Thessalonians 1:9

IDOLS

Keep your lives free from the love of money.

Hebrews 13:5

People who want to get rich fall into temptation and a trap and into many foolish and harmful desires that plunge men into ruin and destruction.

1 Timothy 6:9

Whoever loves money never has money enough; whoever loves wealth is never satisfied with his income.

Ecclesiastes 5:10

Keep yourselves from idols.

1 John 5:21

Everyone who competes in the games goes into strict training. They do it to get a crown that will not last; but we do it to get a crown that will last forever.

1 Corinthians 9:25

"Why spend money on what is not bread, and your labor on what does not satisfy? Listen, listen to me, and eat what is good, and your soul will delight in the richest of fare," declares the LORD.

Isaiah 55:2

IDOLS

During the best years of my active basketball—playing life, Pete Maravich was always on my mind when I thought about hoops. But what I didn't know at the time was that my hero, "Pistol Pete," was struggling with feelings of inadequacy and defeat. He achieved almost every basketball goal imaginable, but he was empty inside.

Much later, after he left basketball for good, he finally found the answer to happiness: He trusted Christ as Savior.

During the days before Pete became a Christian, he came to realize that all he had accomplished as one of basketball's all-time best players had no lasting meaning. In his book *Pistol Pete: Heir to a Dream*, Pete wrote, "Considering all the so-called good things that had happened in my life, I realized they were almost all brief interludes of ego gratification. Nothing lasted through all the accolades and trophies. I had found nothing to hang on to that would last forever. Even my greatest records would someday be broken. The trophies were collecting dust in the attic."

He discovered what so many others do—that the idols we serve bring us nothing but fleeting happiness. And he "turned to God from idols" (1 Thessalonians 1:9).

Anything that captures our heart is an idol—whether it's a basketball trophy, a multi-million-"dollar contract or anything else. All idols can collect is dust.

JESUS' RETURN

Jesus was taken up before their very eyes, and a cloud hid him from their sight. They were looking intently up into the sky as he was going, when suddenly two men dressed in white stood beside them. "Men of Galilee," they said, "why do you stand here looking into the sky? This same Jesus, who has been taken from you into heaven, will come back in the same way you have seen him go into heaven."

Acts 1:9-11

The Lord himself will come down from heaven, with a loud command, with the voice of the archangel and with the trumpet call of God, and the dead in Christ will rise first. After that, we who are still alive and are left will be caught up together with them in the clouds to meet the Lord in the air. And so we will be with the Lord forever.

1 Thessalonians 4:16-17

Jesus said, "They will see the Son of Man coming on the clouds of the sky, with power and great glory. And he will send his angels with a loud trumpet call, and they will gather his elect from the four winds, from one end of the heavens to the other."

Matthew 24:30-31

JESUS' RETURN

I saw heaven standing open and there before me was a white horse, whose rider is called Faithful and True. With justice he judges and makes war. His eyes are like blazing fire, and on his head are many crowns.... On his robe and on his thigh he has this name written: KING OF KINGS AND LORD OF LORDS.

Revelation 19:11-12, 16

"As surely as I live," says the Lord,
"every knee will bow before me;
    every tongue will confess to God."

Romans 14:11

Jesus said, "As lightning that comes from the east is visible even in the west, so will be the coming of the Son of Man."

Matthew 24:27

Jesus said, "Behold, I am coming soon! My reward is with me, and I will give to everyone according to what he has done. I am the Alpha and the Omega, the First and the Last, the Beginning and the End."

Revelation 22:12-13

JESUS' RETURN

Jesus said, "As it was in the days of Noah, so it will be at the coming of the Son of Man. For in the days before the flood, people were eating and drinking, marrying and giving in marriage, up to the day Noah entered the ark; and they knew nothing about what would happen until the flood came and took them all away. That is how it will be at the coming of the Son of Man. Two men will be in the field; one will be taken and the other left. Two women will be grinding with a hand mill; one will be taken and the other left. Therefore, keep watch, because you do not know on what day your Lord will come. But understand this: If the owner of the house had known at what time of night the thief was coming, he would have kept watch and would not have let his house be broken into. So you also must be ready, because the Son of Man will come at an hour when you do not expect him."

Matthew 24:37-44

JESUS' RETURN

Help is on the way.

That's what every sports team wants to hear. It could come in the form of a number one draft pick who will ride onto the scene and give the team instant credibility. It could come from a trade in which a team nabs a star from an opponent. And once in a while, help comes when a star makes a great comeback, à la Michael Jordan in 2001 for the Washington Wizards.

With sports teams, that promised boost sometimes does not materialize—even from a superstar. The Washington Wizards got Jordan back but were still not a championship team. In sports, you just don't know for sure if true help is on the way.

Not so with Jesus. In Revelation 22:7, he promised that he is going to return. And when he does, there is no doubt about the outcome. Jesus' come-back will not be met with mediocrity or defeat. He will bring ultimate victory. He will create a new world of glory, majesty, praise and joy.

"Behold, I am coming soon!" he said (Revelation 22:7). Those words can become our source of strength and hope. They can calm our hearts and fill our souls with confidence. We know that Jesus' return will bring a victory that we will celebrate, not just for a season, but for ever and ever.

LEADERSHIP

Follow my example, as I follow the example of Christ.

1 Corinthians 11:1

If anyone sets his heart on being an overseer, he desires a noble task. Now the overseer must be above reproach, the husband of but one wife, temperate, self-controlled, respectable, hospitable, able to teach, not given to drunkenness, not violent but gentle, not quarrelsome, not a lover of money. He must manage his own family well and see that his children obey him with proper respect.

1 Timothy 3:1-4

Deacons, likewise, are to be men worthy of respect, sincere, not indulging in much wine, and not pursuing dishonest gain. They must keep hold of the deep truths of the faith with a clear con-science.

1 Timothy 3:8-9

If a man's gift is ... leadership, let him govern diligently.

Romans 12:6-8

LEADERSHIP

The LORD told Joshua, "Be strong and courageous, because you will lead these people to inherit the land I swore to their forefathers to give them. Be strong and very courageous. Be careful to obey all the law my servant Moses gave you; do not turn from it to the right or to the left, that you may be successful wherever you go. Do not let this Book of the Law depart from your mouth; meditate on it day and night, so that you may be careful to do everything written in it. Then you will be prosperous and successful."

Joshua 1:6, 8

You must teach what is in accord with sound doctrine. Teach the older men to be temperate, worthy of respect, self-controlled, and sound in faith, in love and in endurance. Likewise, teach the older women to be reverent in the way they live, not to be slanderers or addicted to much wine, but to teach what is good. Then they can train the younger women to love their husbands and children, to be self-controlled and pure, to be busy at home, to be kind, and to be subject to their husbands, so that no one will malign the word of God. Similarly, encourage the young men to be self-controlled. In everything set them an example by doing what is good. In your teaching show integrity, seriousness and soundness of speech that cannot be condemned.

Titus 2:1-8

LEADERSHIP

Jesus said, "If anyone wants to be first, he must be the very last, and the servant of all."

Mark 9:35

Jesus said, "The greatest among you will be your servant. For whoever exalts himself will be humbled, and whoever humbles himself will be exalted."

Matthew 23:11-12

Moses was a very humble man, more humble than anyone else on the face of the earth.

Numbers 12:3

Humility comes before honor.

Proverbs 15:33

Do not think of yourself more highly than you ought, but rather think of yourself with sober judgment, in accordance with the measure of faith God has given you.

Romans 12:3

Jesus said, "He who is least among you all—he is the greatest."

Luke 9:48

LEADERSHIP

Jesus said, "The greatest among you should be like the youngest, and the one who rules like the one who serves. For who is greater, the one who is at the table or the one who serves? Is it not the one who is at the table? But I am among you as one who serves."

Luke 22:26-27

"Let not the wise man boast of his wisdom
    or the strong man boast of his strength
    or the rich man boast of his riches,
but let him who boasts boast about this:
    that he understands and knows me,"
        declares the LORD.

Jeremiah 9:23-24

Moses said to the LORD, "You have been telling me, 'Lead these people,' but you have not let me know whom you will send with me. You have said, 'I know you by name and you have found favor with me.' If you are pleased with me, teach me your ways so I may know you and continue to find favor with you. Remember that this nation is your people." The LORD replied, "My Presence will go with you, and I will give you rest."

Exodus 33:12-14

Give me wisdom and knowledge, that I may lead.

2 Chronicles 1:10

LEADERSHIP

Set an example for the believers in speech, in life, in love, in faith and in purity.

1 Timothy 4:12

You yourselves know how you ought to follow our example. We were not idle when we were with you, nor did we eat anyone's food without paying for it. On the contrary, we worked night and day, laboring and toiling so that we would not be a burden to any of you. We did this, not because we do not have the right to such help, but in order to make ourselves a model for you to follow.

2 Thessalonians 3:7-9

The king is to write for himself on a scroll a copy of this law, taken from that of the priests, who are Levites. It is to be with him, and he is to read it all the days of his life so that he may learn to revere the LORD his God and follow carefully all the words of this law and these decrees and not consider himself better than his brothers and turn from the law to the right or to the left.

Deuteronomy 17:18-20

Devotional Thought on

LEADERSHIP

In recalling my college years on the basketball floor, I was reminded that I was greatly affected by the leadership of my coach. And his help encompassed so much more than what he taught me on the basketball court.

When I think of Dr. Don Callan, the words of Hebrews 13:7, 17 are apropos: "Remember your leaders, who spoke the word of God to you. Consider the outcome of their way of life and imitate their faith.... They keep watch over you as men who must give an account."

Indeed, Coach was that kind of leader. He shared God's Word with us. And he proved his concern for me by maintaining an interest in my career long after the statute of limitations expired on my playing days.

Leaders. Are you one? If so, be the kind the writer of Hebrews was talking about. Disseminate the truths of Scripture in both word and deed. Compose a way of life that is worthy of imitation. Use your authority wisely. Observe and guide those who must answer to you.

On the other hand, if you are under the guidance of godly leaders, learn from them and follow their instruction. In the days and years to come, you'll be glad you did. And someday you'll "remember your leaders" and thank God for what they gave you.

MONUMENTS

Samuel took a stone and set it up between Mizpah and Shen. He named it Ebenezer, saying, "Thus far has the LORD helped us."

1 Samuel 7:12

I will remember the deeds of the LORD;
    yes, I will remember your miracles of long ago.
I will meditate on all your works
    and consider all your mighty deeds.

Psalm 77:11-12

Jacob took the stone he had placed under his head and set it up as a pillar and poured oil on top of it. He called that place Bethel ["House of God"].

Genesis 28:18-19

Since my youth, O God, you have taught me,
    and to this day I declare your marvelous deeds.
Even when I am old and gray,
    do not forsake me, O God,
till I declare your power to the next generation,
    your might to all who are to come.

Psalm 71:17-18

MONUMENTS

Noah came out, together with his sons and his wife and his sons' wives. All the animals and all the creatures that move along the ground and all the birds—everything that moves on the earth—came out of the ark, one kind after another. Then Noah built an altar to the LORD.

Genesis 8:18-20

I will tell of the kindnesses of the LORD,
    the deeds for which he is to be praised,
    according to all the LORD has done for us—
yes, the many good things he has done.

Isaiah 63:7

The LORD appeared to Abram and said, "To your offspring I will give this land." So he built an altar there to the LORD, who had appeared to him.

Genesis 12:7

Be careful, and watch yourselves closely so that you do not forget the things your eyes have seen or let them slip from your heart as long as you live. Teach them to your children and to their children after them.

Deuteronomy 4:9

MONUMENTS

Moses built an altar and called it The LORD is my Banner.

Exodus 17:15

Fix these words of mine in your hearts and minds; tie them as symbols on your hands and bind them on your foreheads. Teach them to your children, talking about them when you sit at home and when you walk along the road, when you lie down and when you get up. Write them on the door-frames of your houses and on your gates, so that your days and the days of your children may be many in the land that the LORD swore to give your forefathers, as many as the days that the heavens are above the earth.

Deuteronomy 11:18-21

The Lord Jesus, on the night he was betrayed, took bread, and when he had given thanks, he broke it and said, "This is my body, which is for you; do this in remembrance of me." In the same way, after supper he took the cup, saying, "This cup is the new covenant in my blood; do this, whenever you drink it, in remembrance of me." For whenever you eat this bread and drink this cup, you proclaim the Lord's death until he comes.

1 Corinthians 11:23-26

MONUMENTS

From the displays in the Women's Basketball Hall of Fame in Knoxville, Tennessee, to the monuments that stand sentry at Yankee Stadium to the statue of Michael Jordan that graces the front entrance to the United Center in Chicago, sports people love to create icons of honor to their heroes.

It's about remembering. Savoring. Cherishing. Recalling.

It's about keeping the memories of our heroes' remarkable achievements before us. The monuments to the outstanding athletes of our time are there so we never forget their greatness.

There's another Jordan monument that we need to think about. It's the assemblage of rocks that the people of Israel plunked down near the Jordan River (Joshua 4:1-9). Each rock represented a different tribe, but the entire mound was to be a symbol—a marking that would remind the people of God's greatness. Those rocks would stand forever at that spot as a reminder of what God had done to deliver his people.

What kind of monuments are we building in our lives and in the lives of our families? Are there markers—made of memories rather than stone— that help our families recall God's goodness, provision, love and intervention?

MOTIVATION

Let us consider how we may spur one another on toward love and good deeds.

Hebrews 10:24

Warn those who are idle, encourage the timid, help the weak, be patient with everyone.

1 Thessalonians 5:14

The sluggard craves and gets nothing,
   but the desires of the diligent are fully satisfied.

Proverbs 13:4

Encourage and rebuke with all authority.

Titus 2:15

In the presence of God and of Christ Jesus, who will judge the living and the dead, and in view of his appearing and his kingdom, I give you this charge: Preach the Word; be prepared in season and out of season; correct, rebuke and encourage—with great patience and careful instruction.

2 Timothy 4:1-2

Encourage one another daily, as long as it is called Today.

Hebrews 3:13

MOTIVATION

We want each of you to show this same diligence to the very end, in order to make your hope sure. We do not want you to become lazy, but to imitate those who through faith and patience inherit what has been promised.

Hebrews 6:11-12

Encourage one another and build each other up.

1 Thessalonians 5:11

Do not throw away your confidence; it will be richly rewarded. You need to persevere so that when you have done the will of God, you will receive what he has promised.

Hebrews 10:35-36

The LORD himself goes before you and will be with you; he will never leave you nor forsake you. Do not be afraid; do not be discouraged.

Deuteronomy 31:8

We always thank God for all of you, mentioning you in our prayers. We continually remember before our God and Father your work produced by faith, your labor prompted by love, and your endurance inspired by hope in our Lord Jesus Christ.

1 Thessalonians 1:2-3

MOTIVATION

*I press on to take hold of that for which Christ
Jesus took hold of me. Brothers, I do not consider
myself yet to have taken hold of it. But one thing I
do: Forgetting what is behind and straining toward
what is ahead, I press on toward the goal to win
the prize for which God has called me heavenward
in Christ Jesus.*

Philippians 3:12-14

Let us acknowledge the LORD;
   let us press on to acknowledge him.
As surely as the sun rises,
   he will appear;
he will come to us like the winter rains,
   like the spring rains that water the earth.

Hosea 6:3

*Jesus said, "Well done, good and faithful servant!
You have been faithful with a few things; I will put
you in charge of many things. Come and share
your master's happiness!"*

Matthew 25:21

MOTIVATION

Whatever the God of heaven has prescribed, let it be done with diligence for the temple of the God of heaven.

Ezra 7:23

Blessed are all who fear the LORD,
 who walk in his ways.
You will eat the fruit of your labor;
 blessings and prosperity will be yours.

Psalm 128:1-2

It is good and proper for a man to eat and drink, and to find satisfaction in his toilsome labor under the sun during the few days of life God has given him-for this is his lot. Moreover, when God gives any man wealth and possessions, and enables him to enjoy them, to accept his lot and be happy in his work—this is a gift of God.

Ecclesiastes 5:18-19

May the favor of the Lord our God rest upon us;
 establish the work of our hands for us—
 yes, establish the work of our hands.

Psalm 90:17

MOTIVATION

Let us encourage one another—and all the more as you see the Day approaching.

Hebrews 10:25

May the Lord direct your hearts into God's love and Christ's perseverance.

2 Thessalonians 3:5

Let us not become weary in doing good, for at the proper time we will reap a harvest if we do not give up.

Galatians 6:9

Hope does not disappoint us, because God has poured out his love into our hearts by the Holy Spirit, whom he has given us.

Romans 5:5

Never tire of doing what is right.

2 Thessalonians 3:13

May our Lord Jesus Christ himself and God our Father, who loved us and by his grace gave us eternal encouragement and good hope, encourage your hearts and strengthen you in every good deed and word.

2 Thessalonians 2:16-17

MOTIVATION

As a high school basketball coach, one of my most important jobs was motivation. It was up to me, I felt, to motivate my players to work hard, both during the season and in the off-season.

Some players got the hint. Several of my players went from being mediocre athletes to being very good athletes because they filled in the shot charts I asked them to keep during the off-season, shooting thousands of shots.

For one young man, though, I didn't get the point across. As a junior, he started and played quite well. But in the long layoff between the end of one season and the beginning of the next, he didn't work. He had no one overseeing him, and he was not wise. So, when his senior year rolled around, he found himself on the bench far more than he wanted to be.

Laziness and lack of initiative do not breed happiness. Solomon's illustration of the ant is clear. When God tells us to "consider its ways and be wise" (Proverbs 6:6), God is telling us to be active people, not lazy people who wait for others to either meet their needs or give them something they haven't earned.

God, who made not only the ant, but us as well, knows what will make us the most successful in life's challenges.

OFFENSE

Jesus said, "Go and make disciples of all nations, baptizing them in the name of the Father and of the Son and of the Holy Spirit, and teaching them to obey everything I have commanded you. And surely I am with you always, to the very end of the age."

Matthew 28:19-20

How, then, can they call on the one they have not believed in? And how can they believe in the one of whom they have not heard? And how can they hear without someone preaching to them? And how can they preach unless they are sent? As it is written, "How beautiful are the feet of those who bring good news!"

Romans 10:14-15

I consider my life worth nothing to me, if only I may finish the race and complete the task the Lord Jesus has given me—the task of testifying to the gospel of God's grace.

Acts 20:24

Jesus said, "This gospel of the kingdom will be preached in the whole world as a testimony to all nations."

Matthew 24:14

OFFENSE

Do not be ashamed to testify about our Lord.

2 Timothy 1:8

Jesus told them many things in parables, saying: "A farmer went out to sow his seed. As he was scattering the seed, some fell along the path, and the birds came and ate it up. Some fell on rocky places, where it did not have much soil. It sprang up quickly, because the soil was shallow. But when the sun came up, the plants were scorched, and they withered because they had no root. Other seed fell among thorns, which grew up and choked the plants. Still other seed fell on good soil, where it produced a crop—a hundred, sixty or thirty times what was sown."

Matthew 13:3-8

The Lord has assigned to each his task. I planted the seed, Apollos watered it, but God made it grow. So neither he who plants nor he who waters is anything, but only God, who makes things grow. The man who plants and the man who waters have one purpose, and each will be rewarded according to his own labor. For we are God's fellow workers.

1 Corinthians 3:5-9

I am not ashamed of the gospel, because it is the power of God for the salvation of everyone who believes.

Romans 1:16

OFFENSE

By the grace God has given me, I laid a foundation as an expert builder, and someone else is building on it. But each one should be careful how he builds. For no one can lay any foundation other than the one already laid, which is Jesus Christ. If any man builds on this foundation using gold, silver, costly stones, wood, hay or straw, his work will be shown for what it is, because the Day will bring it to light. It will be revealed with fire, and the fire will test the quality of each man's work. If what he has built survives, he will receive his reward.

1 Corinthians 3:10-14

Jesus said, "Do not worry beforehand about what to say. Just say whatever is given you at the time, for it is not you speaking, but the Holy Spirit."

Mark 13:11

Pray also for me, that whenever I open my mouth, words may be given me so that I will fearlessly make known the mystery of the gospel.

Ephesians 6:19

Jesus said, "You will receive power when the Holy Spirit comes on you; and you will be my witnesses in Jerusalem, and in all Judea and Samaria, and to the ends of the earth."

Acts 1:8

OFFENSE

The summer after I graduated from college, I took a road trip that was even longer than the queen of Sheba's. On a basketball evangelism team called Athletes for Christ, my teammates and I crossed the Pacific Ocean and landed on a tiny spot of land called Luzon, the Philippines.

Like the queen, who had heard a lot about Solomon, we had heard a lot about the people of the Philippines. The queen discovered that what she had heard was correct: Solomon was wise and rich. We discovered, as we had been told, that the people of that island nation were kindhearted and warm.

The queen said to Solomon, "You have far exceeded the report I heard" (2 Chronicles 9:6). For our part, we discovered that the beauty of the Philippines far outstripped our imagination of it.

It is such a great idea for young people to take trips such as the one I mentioned above. Traveling to, and living in, a land so different from the one in which we grew up gives us a clearer understanding of the people and culture than we would otherwise have.

If you get a chance, take a road trip. Seek a new land to visit so that you can tell others about Jesus and can learn about the lives of others.

PLAYING THROUGH PAIN

[Trials] have come so that your faith—of greater worth than gold, which perishes even though refined by fire—may be proved genuine and may result in praise, glory and honor when Jesus Christ is revealed.

1 Peter 1:7

The apostles left the Sanhedrin, rejoicing because they had been counted worthy of suffering disgrace for the Name. Day after day, in the temple courts and from house to house, they never stopped teaching and proclaiming the good news that Jesus is the Christ.

Acts 5:41-42

Suffering produces perseverance; perseverance, character; and character, hope.

Romans 5:3-4

Do not be surprised at the painful trial you are suffering, as though something strange were happening to you. But rejoice that you participate in the sufferings of Christ, so that you may be overjoyed when his glory is revealed. If you are insulted because of the name of Christ, you are blessed, for the Spirit of glory and of God rests on you.... If you suffer as a Christian, do not be ashamed, but praise God that you bear that name.

1 Peter 4:12-14, 16

PLAYING THROUGH PAIN

As an example of patience in the face of suffering, take the prophets who spoke in the name of the Lord. As you know, we consider blessed those who have persevered. You have heard of Job's perseverance and have seen what the Lord finally brought about. The Lord is full of compassion and mercy.

James 5:10-11

Join with me in suffering for the gospel, by the power of God, who has saved us and called us to a holy life—not because of anything we have done but because of his own purpose and grace. This grace was given us in Christ Jesus before the beginning of time, but it has now been revealed through the appearing of our Savior, Christ Jesus, who has destroyed death and has brought life and immortality to light through the gospel. And of this gospel I was appointed a herald and an apostle and a teacher. That is why I am suffering as I am. Yet I am not ashamed, because I know whom I have believed, and am convinced that he is able to guard what I have entrusted to him for that day.

2 Timothy 1:8-12

PLAYING THROUGH PAIN

Among God's churches we boast about your perseverance and faith in all the persecutions and trials you are enduring. All this is evidence that God's judgment is right, and as a result you will be counted worthy of the kingdom of God, for which you are suffering. God is just: He will pay back trouble to those who trouble you and give relief to you who are troubled.

2 Thessalonians 1:4-7

These are they who have come out of the great tribulation; they have washed their robes and made them white in the blood of the Lamb. Therefore,

"they are before the throne of God
    and serve him day and night in his temple;
and he who sits on the throne will spread his
tent over them.
Never again will they hunger;
    never again will they thirst.
The sun will not beat upon them,
    nor any scorching heat.
For the Lamb at the center of the throne will be
their shepherd;
    he will lead them to springs of living water.
And God will wipe away every tear from their
eyes."

Revelation 7:14-17

PLAYING THROUGH PAIN

Many athletes have turned to faith in Jesus Christ while in the middle of their playing careers. In baseball, Gary Gaetti, Walt Weiss and Tony Clark were all veteran athletes when they came to faith in Christ; in hoops, there's Hersey Hawkins; in hockey, there's John Vanbiesbrouck.

It was not always easy for these players when they began doing good—when they began their new lives in Christ. Sometimes, they had to suffer because of their efforts. For instance, Gary Gaetti was a member of the Minnesota Twins when he became a believer. Before Gaetti's transformation, he and his buddy Kent Hrbek spent a lot of time together. Much of that time was spent drinking. You'd think fans in Minnesota would appreciate the fact that their star middle infielder was no longer getting drunk and could now concentrate on baseball. On the contrary, they thought Gaetti's new interest in right living made him a soft baseball player, so they and the media began to criticize him. It wasn't long before Gaetti wanted to get out of Minnesota.

Sometimes when we do what is right, we get treated wrong.

Have you suffered for doing what is right? That's great! According to Peter, if that happens, then you are "blessed" (1 Peter 3:14). You are privileged in God's eyes for you have suffered for his name.

PRAISE

I will extol the LORD at all times;
　　his praise will always be on my lips.
My soul will boast in the LORD;
　　let the afflicted hear and rejoice.
Glorify the LORD with me;
　　let us exalt his name together.

Psalm 34:1-3

Sing to the LORD a new song;
　　sing to the LORD, all the earth.
Sing to the LORD, praise his name;
　　proclaim his salvation day after day.
Declare his glory among the nations,
　　his marvelous deeds among all peoples.

Psalm 96:1-3

Because your love is better than life, O LORD,
　　my lips will glorify you.
I will praise you as long as I live,
　　and in your name I will lift up my hands.
My soul will be satisfied as with the richest of foods;
　　with singing lips my mouth will praise you.

Psalm 63:3-5

PRAISE

Shout with joy to God, all the earth!
Sing the glory of his name;
  make his praise glorious!
Say to God, "How awesome are your deeds!…
All the earth bows down to you;
  they sing praise to you,
  they sing praise to your name."

Psalm 66:1-4

Not to us, O Lord, not to us
  but to your name be the glory,
  because of your love and faithfulness.

Psalm 115:1

Give thanks to the Lord, call on his name;
  make known among the nations what he has done.
Sing to him, sing praise to him;
  tell of all his wonderful acts.
Glory in his holy name;
  let the hearts of those who seek the Lord rejoice.

Psalm 105:1-3

PRAISE

The LORD is my strength and my song;
    he has become my salvation.
He is my God, and I will praise him,
    my father's God, and I will exalt him.

Exodus 15:2

I will proclaim the name of the LORD.
    Oh, praise the greatness of our God!
He is the Rock, his works are perfect,
    and all his ways are just.
A faithful God who does no wrong,
    upright and just is he.

Deuteronomy 32:3-4

*Give glory to the LORD, the God of Israel, and give
him the praise.*

Joshua 7:19

PRAISE

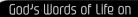

O Lord, you are my God;
  I will exalt you and praise your name,
for in perfect faithfulness
  you have done marvelous things,
  things planned long ago.

Isaiah 25:1

Praise be to the Lord, the God of Israel,
  because he has come and has redeemed his
people.

Luke 1:68

*May the glory of the Lord be praised in his
dwelling place!*

Ezekiel 3:12

*Praise be to the God and Father of our Lord Jesus
Christ, the Father of compassion and the God of all
comfort.*

2 Corinthians 1:3

*Through Jesus ... let us continually offer to God a
sacrifice of praise—the fruit of lips that confess his
name.*

Hebrews 13:15

PRAISE

I will praise God's name in song
  and glorify him with thanksgiving.

Psalm 69:30

Great and marvelous are your deeds,
  Lord God Almighty.
Just and true are your ways,
  King of the ages.
Who will not fear you, O Lord,
  and bring glory to your name?
For you alone are holy.
All nations will come
  and worship before you,
for your righteous acts have been revealed.

Revelation 15:3-4

I will praise you, O Lord my God, with all my heart;
  I will glorify your name forever.
For great is your love toward me.

Psalm 86:12-13

PRAISE

Christian athletes have shown over the years that they can find a variety of ways to praise God and thank him for his help.

For example, NBA assists expert Mark Jackson sometimes crosses his forearms to indicate the cross after he makes a basket.

In the middle of the hard work of writing his prophetic book, Isaiah paused for praise as well. In Isaiah 25, he set aside a portion of Scripture to bring his praises to God. He begins with words that have come to be favorite praise words of millions of believers: "O LORD, you are my God; I will exalt you and praise your name" (Isaiah 25:1).

He praised God's power (verse 2), his compassion (verse 4) and his future provision (verses 6-8). Isaiah said, "Surely this is our God; we trusted in him, and he saved us" (verse 9).

In the middle of whatever we are doing—whether it is competing in a sport, running a business, going to school, raising a family or enjoying retirement—how often do we stop and praise God? How often do we simply turn our thoughts toward him and say, "O LORD, you are my God" (Isaiah 25:1)?

If our hearts overflow as Isaiah's did, praise will be a natural part of our lives.

PRAYER

Pray in the Spirit on all occasions with all kinds of prayers and requests. With this in mind, be alert and always keep on praying for all the saints.

Ephesians 6:18

Jesus said, "When you pray, go into your room, close the door and pray to your Father, who is unseen. Then your Father, who sees what is done in secret, will reward you."

Matthew 6:6

The LORD is near to all who call on him,
   to all who call on him in truth.
He fulfills the desires of those who fear him;
   he hears their cry and saves them.

Psalm 145:18-19

Jesus often withdrew to lonely places and prayed.

Luke 5:16

In my distress I called to the LORD,
   and he answered me.
From the depths of the grave I called for help,
   and you listened to my cry.

Jonah 2:2

PRAYER

Jesus said, "Your Father knows what you need before you ask him."

Matthew 6:8

Know that the LORD has set apart the godly for himself;
> the LORD will hear when I call to him.

Psalm 4:3

Another angel, who had a golden censer, came and stood at the altar. He was given much incense to offer, with the prayers of all the saints, on the golden altar before the throne. The smoke of the incense, together with the prayers of the saints, went up before God from the angel's hand.

Revelation 8:3-4

During the days of Jesus' life on earth, he offered up prayers and petitions with loud cries and tears to the one who could save him from death, and he was heard because of his reverent submission.

Hebrews 5:7

Jesus said, "Ask and it will be given to you; seek and you will find; knock and the door will be opened to you. For everyone who asks receives; he who seeks finds; and to him who knocks, the door will be opened."

Matthew 7:7-8

PRAYER

God heard them, for their prayer reached heaven, his holy dwelling place.

Answer me when I call to you,
    O my righteous God.
Give me relief from my distress;
    be merciful to me and hear my prayer.

Psalm 4:1

The LORD our God is near us whenever we pray to him.

Deuteronomy 4:7

God answered their prayers, because they trusted in him.

1 Chronicles 5:20

If I had cherished sin in my heart,
    the Lord would not have listened;
but God has surely listened
    and heard my voice in prayer.
Praise be to God,
    who has not rejected my prayer
    or withheld his love from me!

Psalm 66:18-20

PRAYER

O LORD, let everyone who is godly pray to you
while you may be found.

Psalm 32:6

Hear my prayer, O LORD;
listen to my cry for mercy.
In the day of my trouble I will call to you,
for you will answer me.

Psalm 86:6-7

O LORD, I call to you; come quickly to me.
Hear my voice when I call to you.
May my prayer be set before you like incense;
may the lifting up of my hands be like the
evening sacrifice.

Psalm 141:1-2

The LORD … hears the prayer of the righteous.

Proverbs 15:29

*Very early in the morning, while it was still dark,
Jesus got up, left the house and went off to a soli-
tary place, where he prayed.*

Mark 1:35

PRAYER

The prayer of a righteous man is powerful and effective. Elijah was a man just like us. He prayed earnestly that it would not rain, and it did not rain on the land for three and a half years. Again he prayed, and the heavens gave rain, and the earth produced its crops.

James 5:16-18

Jesus said, "Which of you, if his son asks for bread, will give him a stone? Or if he asks for a fish, will give him a snake? If you ... know how to give good gifts to your children, how much more will your Father in heaven give good gifts to those who ask him!"

Matthew 7:9-11

Jesus said, "This, then, is how you should pray:

'Our Father in heaven,
hallowed be your name,
your kingdom come,
your will be done
   on earth as it is in heaven.
Give us today our daily bread.
Forgive us our debts,
   as we also have forgiven our debtors.
And lead us not into temptation,
but deliver us from the evil one.'"

Matthew 6:9-13

Devotional Thought on
PRAYER

The apostle Paul was not shy about asking the people to whom he wrote to pray for him. After giving them some clear instructions, he then gave the people of Thessalonica some specific prayer requests.

Let's look at what some athletes told me when I asked them what kinds of requests were on their hearts.

A pro basketball player: "Growth in my relationship with Jesus. That my actions will show evidence of the One who lives within me. Wisdom and discernment. Physical health and safety."

A triathlete: "Whether in winning or losing, present a Christlike character so God may receive the glory."

A major league infielder: "That we maintain a solid gospel presentation on and off the field with our actions, words and deeds. That we are protected from the temptations every believer encounters."

Paul asked for prayer that the message of the Lord would spread and that he and his colleagues would be delivered from evil men. That's not too different from the athletes I talked with.

Whose names are on your prayer list? It is vital that we keep praying for our fellow believers—asking that God protect them and that they be able to continue the task of spreading the gospel.

PRIORITIES

Jesus said, "Do not worry, saying, 'What shall we eat?' or 'What shall we drink?' or 'What shall we wear?' For [unbelievers] run after all these things, and your heavenly Father knows that you need them. But seek first his kingdom and his righteousness, and all these things will be given to you as well."

Matthew 6:31-33

What I received I passed on to you as of first importance: that Christ died for our sins according to the Scriptures, that he was buried, that he was raised on the third day according to the Scriptures, and that he appeared to Peter, and then to the Twelve.

1 Corinthians 15:3-5

An expert in the law ... tested Jesus with this question: "Teacher, which is the greatest commandment in the Law?" Jesus replied: "'Love the Lord your God with all your heart and with all your soul and with all your mind.' This is the first and greatest commandment. And the second is like it: 'Love your neighbor as yourself.' All the Law and the Prophets hang on these two commandments."

Matthew 22:35-40

The important thing is that in every way ... Christ is preached.

Philippians 1:18

PRIORITIES

Jesus said, "If anyone would come after me, he must deny himself and take up his cross and follow me. For whoever wants to save his life will lose it, but whoever loses his life for me will find it. What good will it be for a man if he gains the whole world, yet forfeits his soul? Or what can a man give in exchange for his soul?"

Matthew 16:24-26

Whatever was to my profit I now consider loss for the sake of Christ. What is more, I consider every-thing a loss compared to the surpassing greatness of knowing Christ Jesus my Lord.

Philippians 3:7-8

The disciples came to Jesus and asked, "Who is the greatest in the kingdom of heaven?" He called a lit-tle child and had him stand among them. And he said: "I tell you the truth, unless you change and become like little children, you will never enter the kingdom of heaven. Therefore, whoever humbles himself like this child is the greatest in the kingdom of heaven."

Matthew 18:1-4

PRIORITIES

Jesus said, "I am the First and the Last."

Revelation 1:17

Jesus is the image of the invisible God, the first-born over all creation. For by him all things were created: things in heaven and on earth, visible and invisible, whether thrones or powers or rulers or authorities; all things were created by him and for him. He is before all things, and in him all things hold together. And he is the head of the body, the church; he is the beginning and the firstborn from among the dead, so that in everything he might have the supremacy.

Colossians 1:15-18

God made known to us the mystery of his will according to his good pleasure, which he purposed in Christ, to be put into effect when the times will have reached their fulfillment—to bring all things in heaven and on earth together under one head, even Christ.

Ephesians 1:9-10

You, O LORD, are the Most High over all the earth;

you are exalted far above all gods.

Psalm 97:9

PRIORITIES

Take it from a two-sport man, something has to have top place in your life.

When Charlie Ward was in college at Florida State University, he was not only a Heisman Trophy-winning football player, but he was also a pretty good basketball player for the Seminoles.

Surprisingly, it was in basketball that he became famous as a professional, having some very productive years in the NBA with the New York Knicks.

But Charlie Ward knows that although a person may have a couple of different interests it is important for one thing to have top priority. "It's always good to have Christ in your life first and foremost," he says, "because once you have him first, everything else is something he's blessed you with, something extra."

Here's how Jesus stated that principle in the Sermon on the Mount: "No one can serve two masters. Either he will hate the one and love the other, or he will be devoted to the one and despise the other" (Matthew 6:24). In no situation are we to put anything before God. We cannot serve God and something we put before him.

Life is about putting first things first. And that first thing must be God. "Keep things prioritized, and everything will be fine," Charlie Ward reminds us.

TEAMMATES

There is a friend who sticks closer than a brother.

Proverbs 18:24

Two are better than one,
    because they have a good return for their work:
If one falls down,
    his friend can help him up.
But pity the man who falls
    and has no one to help him up!...
Though one may be overpowered,
    two can defend themselves.
A cord of three strands is not quickly broken.

Ecclesiastes 4:9, 12

Jonathan became one in spirit with David, and he loved him as himself.

1 Samuel 18:1

As iron sharpens iron,
    so one man sharpens another.

Proverbs 27:17

TEAMMATES

A righteous man is cautious in friendship.

Proverbs 12:26

Do not be yoked together with unbelievers. For what do righteousness and wickedness have in common? Or what fellowship can light have with darkness? What harmony is there between Christ and Belial? What does a believer have in common with an unbeliever?

2 Corinthians 6:14-15

He who walks with the wise grows wise.

Proverbs 13:20

Jonathan said to David, "Go in peace, for we have sworn friendship with each other in the name of the LORD, saying, 'The LORD is witness between you and me, and between your descendants and my descendants forever.'"

1 Samuel 20:42

If we walk in the light, as he is in the light, we have fellowship with one another.

1 John 1:7

TEAMMATES

If you have any encouragement from being united with Christ, if any comfort from his love, if any fellowship with the Spirit, if any tenderness and compassion, then make my joy complete by being like-minded, having the same love, being one in spirit and purpose.

Philippians 2:1-2

I appeal to you, brothers, in the name of our Lord Jesus Christ, that all of you agree with one another so that there may be no divisions among you and that you may be perfectly united in mind and thought.

1 Corinthians 1:10

My purpose is that they may be encouraged in heart and united in love, so that they may have the full riches of complete understanding, in order that they may know the mystery of God, namely, Christ, in whom are hidden all the treasures of wisdom and knowledge.

Colossians 2:2-3

May the God who gives endurance and encouragement give you a spirit of unity among yourselves as you follow Christ Jesus, so that with one heart and mouth you may glorify the God and Father of our Lord Jesus Christ.

Romans 15:5-6

TEAMMATES

Avery Johnson and David Robinson, who together won the NBA crown with the San Antonio Spurs in 1999, could very easily be a modern-day equivalent of Jonathan and David (1 Samuel 20). They grew to be very close friends who both loved the Lord and wanted to please him as they together played on a basketball team that struggled to get to a place many people said they would never go: the NBA championship.

David and Avery were friends who learned to lean on each other and on God for help. David Robinson said of their friendship: "Our faith is the foundation of our friendship. That's why our friendship has stood the test of time. We had each other for encouragement. We knew that fellowship was a critical part of our growth as Christians."

It's not often that we find such true friendship. But when we do, we know we have something special from God: Someone to hold us accountable. Someone to encourage us. Someone to spur (pun intended) us on to be a better person than we would be alone.

If you do not have that kind of friendship with someone, ask the Lord for a friend like Jonathan was to David. When two people share the common goal of serving the Lord, they both can achieve grand things for God.

TEAMWORK

Just as each of us has one body with many members, and these members do not all have the same function, so in Christ we who are many form one body, and each member belongs to all the others. We have different gifts, according to the grace given us.

Romans 12:4-6

If the ear should say, "Because I am not an eye, I do not belong to the body," it would not for that reason cease to be part of the body. If the whole body were an eye, where would the sense of hearing be? If the whole body were an ear, where would the sense of smell be? But in fact God has arranged the parts in the body, every one of them, just as he wanted them to be… God has combined the members of the body and has given greater honor to the parts that lacked it, so that there should be no division in the body, but that its parts should have equal concern for each other. If one part suffers, every part suffers with it; if one part is honored, every part rejoices with it.

1 Corinthians 12:16-18, 24-26

Each one should use whatever gift he has received to serve others, faithfully administering God's grace in its various forms.

1 Peter 4:10

TEAMWORK

Carry each other's burdens, and in this way you will fulfill the law of Christ.

Galatians 6:2

Be devoted to one another in brotherly love. Honor one another above yourselves.... Share with God's people who are in need. Practice hospitality.

Romans 12:10,13

Live in harmony with one another.

Romans 12:16

Let us not become conceited, provoking and envying each other.

Galatians 5:26

Submit to one another out of reverence for Christ.

Ephesians 5:21

Let the word of Christ dwell in you richly as you teach and admonish one another with all wisdom, and as you sing psalms, hymns and spiritual songs with gratitude in your hearts to God.

Colossians 3:16

TEAMWORK

Serve one another in love.

Galatians 5:13

Do nothing out of selfish ambition or vain conceit, but in humility consider others better than your-selves. Each of you should look not only to your own interests, but also to the interests of others.

Philippians 2:3-4

Love one another deeply, from the heart.

1 Peter 1:22

They devoted themselves to the apostles' teaching and to the fellowship, to the breaking of bread and to prayer. Everyone was filled with awe, and many wonders and miraculous signs were done by the apostles. All the believers were together and had everything in common. Selling their possessions and goods, they gave to anyone as he had need. Every day they continued to meet together in the temple courts. They broke bread in their homes and ate together with glad and sincere hearts, praising God and enjoying the favor of all the people. And the Lord added to their number daily those who were being saved.

Acts 2:42-47

Devotional Thought on
TEAMWORK

The toughest job of a youth league coach is to convince all the eager players that they can't all be the pitcher or the quarterback or the goalie. The high-profile positions seem to draw everyone's interest. However, football can't be played with 11 QBs.

And the work of the church can't be accomplished if everyone is the pastor or the deacon or the teacher. According to Paul, God designed his team members to have specific skills. "It was [Christ] who gave some to be apostles, some to be prophets, some to be evangelists, and some to be pastors and teachers" (Ephesians 4:11). Although the people who hold these jobs in the church do different things, they have the same goal: to build up the body of believers until they "reach unity in the faith and in the knowledge of the Son of God" (verse 13).

These jobs are diverse positions with differing functions, but the people who hold them all work toward the same thing. It sounds like a description of very successful sports teams such as the powerful Chicago Bulls of the Michael Jordan-Scottie Pippen era.

When the people on a sports team stick to their jobs and do them well, things happen—good things. And the same is true in a church.

TIMES OF TROUBLE

Jesus said, "In this world you will have trouble. But take heart! I have overcome the world."

John 16:33

Who shall separate us from the love of Christ? Shall trouble or hardship or persecution or famine or nakedness or danger or sword? ... No, in all these things we are more than conquerors through him who loved us. For I am convinced that neither death nor life, neither angels nor demons, neither the present nor the future, nor any powers, neither height nor depth, nor anything else in all creation, will be able to separate us from the love of God that is in Christ Jesus our Lord.

Romans 8:35, 37-39

Consider it pure joy, my brothers, whenever you face trials of many kinds, because you know that the testing of your faith develops perseverance.

James 1:2-3

A friend loves at all times,
    and a brother is born for adversity.

Proverbs 17:17

TIMES OF TROUBLE

The LORD is a refuge for the oppressed,
a stronghold in times of trouble.
Those who know your name will trust in you,
for you, LORD, have never forsaken those who
seek you.

Psalm 9:9-10

*Do not be afraid. Stand firm and you will see the
deliverance the LORD will bring you today.... The
LORD will fight for you; you need only to be still.*

Exodus 14:13-14

The LORD gives strength to the weary,
and increases the power of the weak.
Even youths grow tired and weary,
and young men stumble and fall;
but those who hope in the LORD
will renew their strength.
They will soar on wings like eagles;
they will run and not grow weary,
they will walk and not be faint.

Isaiah 40:29-31

TIMES OF TROUBLE

*The Lord knows how to rescue godly men
from trials.*

2 Peter 2:9

The LORD is my strength and my shield;
    my heart trusts in him, and I am helped.
My heart leaps for joy
    and I will give thanks to him in song.

Psalm 28:7

We wait in hope for the LORD;
    he is our help and our shield.
In him our hearts rejoice,
    for we trust in his holy name.
May your unfailing love rest upon us, O LORD,
    even as we put our hope in you.

Psalm 33:20-22

The LORD gives strength to his people;
    the LORD blesses his people with peace.

Psalm 29:11

TIMES OF TROUBLE

God is our refuge and strength,
  an ever-present help in trouble.
Therefore we will not fear, though the earth
give way
  and the mountains fall into the heart of the sea,
though its waters roar and foam
  and the mountains quake with their surging.

Psalm 46:1-3

He who dwells in the shelter of the Most High
  will rest in the shadow of the Almighty.
I will say of the LORD, "He is my refuge and my
fortress,
  my God, in whom I trust."

Psalm 91:1-2

*I can do everything through God who gives me
strength.*

Philippians 4:13

O LORD, my strength and my fortress,
  my refuge in time of distress.

Jeremiah 16:19

TIMES OF TROUBLE

In all things God works for the good of those who love him, who have been called according to his purpose.

Romans 8:28

Be strong and courageous. Do not be terrified; do not be discouraged, for the LORD your God will be with you wherever you go.

Joshua 1:9

The righteous man is rescued from trouble.

Proverbs 11:8

Blessed is the man who perseveres under trial, because when he has stood the test, he will receive the crown of life that God has promised to those who love him.

James 1:12

Naked I came from my mother's womb,
    and naked I will depart.
The LORD gave and the LORD has taken away;
    may the name of the LORD be praised.

Job 1:21

Keith Smart made one of the most memorable jump shots in NCAA Final Four history. While playing for Indiana in the final game of the 1987 tournament, Smart hit a shot in the game's waning seconds that gave Indiana the championship over Syracuse.

In 1997 the condominium he and his family lived in burned down. Smart lost his championship ring, his trophies and his video of that famous shot. "We lost everything we owned," Smart told a local newspaper.

But he kept his perspective. "We never have held on to material things. We enjoy what we have, and we have each other," he said, referring to his family. "You just have to get ready to move in the next direction."

Keith Smart successfully passed his adversity training. He faced trouble, and he didn't let it defeat him. He continued to trust God.

Facing adversity and coming out on the other side still standing is what the book of Job is all about. Righteousness did not prevent Job from having trouble, but as things developed over the course of his situation, righteousness was his correct response.

It's important to see beyond the pain and hold onto God's hand until we make it through.

TRAINING

Come, let us go up to the mountain of the LORD,
    to the house of the God of Jacob.
He will teach us his ways,
    so that we may walk in his paths.

Isaiah 2:3

*All Scripture is God-breathed and is useful for
teaching, rebuking, correcting and training in righteousness, so that the man of God may be thor-
oughly equipped for every good work.*

2 Timothy 3:16-17

Show me your ways, O LORD,
    teach me your paths;
guide me in your truth and teach me,
    for you are God my Savior,
    and my hope is in you all day long.

Psalm 25:4-5

I will instruct you and teach you in the way you
should go;
    I will counsel you and watch over you.

Psalm 32:8

TRAINING

Teach me your way, O Lᴏʀᴅ,
  and I will walk in your truth;
give me an undivided heart,
  that I may fear your name.

Psalm 86:11

Deal with your servant according to your love
  and teach me your decrees.
I am your servant; give me discernment
  that I may understand your statutes.

Psalm 119:124-125

Teach me, O Lᴏʀᴅ, to follow your decrees;
  then I will keep them to the end.
Give me understanding, and I will keep your law
  and obey it with all my heart.
Direct me in the path of your commands,
  for there I find delight.

Psalm 119:33-35

Teach me to do your will,
  for you are my God;
may your good Spirit
  lead me on level ground.

Psalm 143:10

TRAINING

Instruct a wise man and he will be wiser still;
    teach a righteous man and he will add to his
learning.

Proverbs 9:9

Your hands made me and formed me, O LORD;
    give me understanding to learn your
commands.

Psalm 119:73

The fear of the LORD is the beginning of wisdom;
    all who follow his precepts have good
understanding.

Psalm 111:10

Jesus said, "The Counselor, the Holy Spirit, whom
the Father will send in my name, will teach you all
things and will remind you of everything I have
said to you."

John 14:26

Everything that was written in the past was written
to teach us, so that through endurance and the
encouragement of the Scriptures we might have
hope.

Romans 15:4

I will praise you with an upright heart, O LORD,
    as I learn your righteous laws.

Psalm 119:7

Devotional Thought on
TRAINING

In 2001 Kwame Brown became the first high school basketball player to be the NBA Number 1 draft choice. But when the Washington Wizards snagged him not long after he graduated from high school, they knew he wouldn't be ready to go up against Shaquille O'Neal or other NBA veterans.

An athlete needs some time to grow into the leading role on a team. That's why Kwame Brown spent a lot of time sitting next to his coaches before he could truly make a difference in the NBA.

Paul had a similar experience soon after he trusted Jesus as his Savior. Before he took a leadership position in the Christian community, he spent considerable time getting prepared.

We all need to spend time with God and with his Word if we want to be effective in service for him. And since it is not practical for us to go off to be alone with God for three years, as Paul appeared to do, we need to develop regular times when we can meet with God.

In effect, we're like Kwame Brown, who had to learn by doing—every day discovering something new and practicing it. We are already in the game—already active in service for God—so we must carve out times for learning, growing and moving closer to God.

TRASH TALK

With the tongue we praise our Lord and Father, and with it we curse men, who have been made in God's likeness. Out of the same mouth come praise and cursing. My brothers, this should not be. Can both fresh water and salt water flow from the same spring? My brothers, can a fig tree bear olives, or a grapevine bear figs? Neither can a salt spring produce fresh water.

James 3:9-12

Do not let any unwholesome talk come out of your mouths, but only what is helpful for building others up according to their needs, that it may benefit those who listen.

Ephesians 4:29

Keep corrupt talk far from your lips.

Proverbs 4:24

Jesus said, "Out of the overflow of the heart the mouth speaks. The good man brings good things out of the good stored up in him, and the evil man brings evil things out of the evil stored up in him. But I tell you that men will have to give account on the day of judgment for every careless word they have spoken. For by your words you will be acquitted, and by your words you will be condemned."

Matthew 12:34-37

TRASH TALK

If anyone is never at fault in what he says, he is a perfect man, able to keep his whole body in check.

James 3:2

An evil man is trapped by his sinful talk,
    but a righteous man escapes trouble.

Proverbs 12:13

Among you there must not be ... obscenity, foolish talk or coarse joking, which are out of place, but rather thanksgiving.

Ephesians 5:3-4

Reckless words pierce like a sword,
    but the tongue of the wise brings healing.

Proverbs 12:18

The goal of this command is love, which comes from a pure heart and a good conscience and a sincere faith. Some have wandered away from these and turned to meaningless talk.

1 Timothy 1:5-6

TRASH TALK

When words are many, sin is not absent,
   but he who holds his tongue is wise.

Proverbs 10:19

A man of knowledge uses words with restraint.

Proverbs 17:27

Words from a wise man's mouth are gracious,
   but a fool is consumed by his own lips.

Ecclesiastes 10:12

He who guards his lips guards his life,
   but he who speaks rashly will come to ruin.

Proverbs 13:3

A man who lacks judgment derides his neighbor,
   but a man of understanding holds his tongue.

Proverbs 11:12

May the words of my mouth and the meditation
of my heart
   be pleasing in your sight,
   O Lord, my Rock and my Redeemer.

Psalm 19:14

TRASH TALK

"I don't particularly like it," says NBA guard Brent Price. "I don't try to partake in that."

Price is discussing trash talk, which is a far-too-common sports phenomenon today. It involves people who have nothing worthwhile to say talking far too much. It's the exchange of sometimes degrading, hurtful words in the name of competition. It's using demeaning words when it might be better to say nothing at all.

"I was always taught," he said, "being a coach's kid, that you go out, play hard, keep your mouth shut, and if you're going to do some damage, do it on the court, not with your mouth. I think some of the trash talk gets out of hand. I think it takes away from the beauty of the game."

In our lives as people who want to please God and honor him, it's never good to put down our neighbor—whether he or she is a co-worker, a friend, a relative, a person in authority or the person you are checking on the soccer pitch. As Price said, "It takes away from the beauty" of interpersonal relationships.

Let's be people of understanding. Let's ask God to guard our lips and hold our tongues. Then, when it comes to how we talk to others, we can "take out" the trash.

VICTORY

The LORD your God himself will fight for you.

Deuteronomy 3:22

"Be still, and know that I am God;
   I will be exalted among the nations,
   I will be exalted in the earth."

The LORD Almighty is with us;
   the God of Jacob is our fortress.

Psalm 46:10-11

*Take up your positions; stand firm and see the
deliverance the LORD will give you.*

2 Chronicles 20:17

*Though we live in the world, we do not wage war
as the world does. The weapons we fight with are
not the weapons of the world. On the contrary,
they have divine power to demolish strongholds.
We demolish arguments and every pretension that
sets itself up against the knowledge of God, and
we take captive every thought to make it obedient
to Christ.*

2 Corinthians 10:3-5

VICTORY

It is God who arms me with strength
  and makes my way perfect.
He makes my feet like the feet of a deer;
  he enables me to stand on the heights.
He trains my hands for battle;
  my arms can bend a bow of bronze.
You give me your shield of victory,
  and your right hand sustains me;
  you stoop down to make me great.

Psalm 18:32–35

*Do not be overcome by evil, but overcome evil
with good.*

Romans 12:21

Shouts of joy and victory
  resound in the tents of the righteous:
  "The LORD's right hand has done mighty
things!"

Psalm 118:15

*They will make war against the Lamb, but the
Lamb will overcome them because he is Lord of
lords and King of kings—and with him will be his
called, chosen and faithful followers.*

Revelation 17:14

VICTORY

You are my lamp, O LORD;
  the LORD turns my darkness into light.
With your help I can advance against a troop;
  with my God I can scale a wall.

2 Samuel 22:29-30

*The LORD your God is the one who goes with you
to fight for you against your enemies to give you
victory.*

Deuteronomy 20:4

*The men of Judah were victorious because they
relied on the LORD, the God of their fathers.*

2 Chronicles 13:18

It was not by their sword that they won the land,
O LORD,
  nor did their arm bring them victory;
it was your right hand, your arm,
  and the light of your face, for you loved them.

Psalm 44:3

The LORD gave David victory wherever he went.

2 Samuel 8:6

VICTORY

David said to [Goliath], "You come against me with sword and spear and javelin, but I come against you in the name of the LORD Almighty, the God of the armies of Israel, whom you have defied. This day the LORD will hand you over to me.... All those gathered here will know that it is not by sword or spear that the LORD saves; for the battle is the LORD's."

1 Samuel 17:45-47

I look for your deliverance, O LORD.

Genesis 49:18

I do not trust in my bow, O LORD,
    my sword does not bring me victory;
but you give us victory over our enemies,
    you put our adversaries to shame.
In God we make our boast all day long,
    and we will praise your name forever.

Psalm 44:6-8

Worship the LORD your God; it is he who will deliver you from the hand of all your enemies.

2 Kings 17:39

VICTORY

The horse is made ready for the day of battle,
  but victory rests with the Lord.

Proverbs 21:31

*You, dear children, are from God and have over-
come them, because the one who is in you is
greater than the one who is in the world.*

1 John 4:4

With God we will gain the victory.

Psalm 60:12

I write to you, young men,
  because you are strong,
  and the word of God lives in you,
  and you have overcome the evil one.

1 John 2:14

*Jesus said, "I have given you authority to ... over-
come all the power of the enemy."*

Luke 10:19

*Thanks be to God! He gives us the victory through
our Lord Jesus Christ.*

1 Corinthians 15:57

VICTORY

Sports people have a wide variety of opinions about winning and losing. For many, to win in sports is the greatest affirmation of importance. To others, it pales in importance compared with other pursuits.

I tend to go along with what the great college basketball coach and statesman John Wooden once said: "I don't know whether always winning is good. It breeds envy and distrust in others and overconfidence and a lack of appreciation very often in those who enjoy it."

So, while winning has its importance in sports, we can see that it should not be, as Red Sanders, Vanderbilt football coach, said, "the only thing."

If we move over into the field of faith and consider what Christ has done for us and what he calls us to do, we must conclude this: We are not just winners by virtue of God's grace—we are more than that.

Paul seems to imply that we will face a multitude of foes on the spiritual battlefield. Among those foes will be those that may try to separate us from Christ's love: trouble, hardship, persecution, famine, nakedness, danger and the sword.

Let's turn our attention toward the battles at hand, and as we do, let's trust our Savior to win them for us. Nothing can stand against him. With him, we are "more than conquerors" (Romans 8:37).

WORSHIP

You are worthy, our Lord and God,
   to receive glory and honor and power,
for you created all things,
   and by your will they were created
   and have their being.

Revelation 4:11

*Since we are receiving a kingdom that cannot be
shaken, let us be thankful, and so worship God
acceptably with reverence and awe, for our "God
is a consuming fire."*

Hebrews 12:28-29

O Lord, our Lord,
   how majestic is your name in all the earth!

Psalm 8:1

Your righteousness reaches to the skies, O God,
   you who have done great things.
   Who, O God, is like you?

Psalm 71:19

I love you, O Lord, my strength.

Psalm 18:1

WORSHIP

Worthy is the Lamb, who was slain,
to receive power and wealth and wisdom and strength
and honor and glory and praise!

Revelation 5:12

All the nations you have made
will come and worship before you, O Lord;
they will bring glory to your name.
For you are great and do marvelous deeds;
you alone are God.

Psalm 86:9-10

Jesus said, "Worship the Lord your God and serve him only."

Luke 4:8

Worship the LORD in the splendor of his holiness;
tremble before him, all the earth.

Psalm 96:9

When Jesus had led his disciples out to the vicinity of Bethany, he lifted up his hands and blessed them. While he was blessing them, he left them and was taken up into heaven. Then they worshiped him and returned to Jerusalem with great joy. And they stayed continually at the temple, praising God.

Luke 24:50-53

WORSHIP

Ascribe to the LORD, O families of nations,
   ascribe to the LORD glory and strength,
   ascribe to the LORD the glory due his name.
Bring an offering and come before him;
   worship the LORD in the splendor of his holiness.

1 Chronicles 16:28-29

*When Solomon finished praying, fire came down
from heaven and consumed the burnt offering and
the sacrifices, and the glory of the LORD filled the
temple. The priests could not enter the temple of
the LORD because the glory of the LORD filled it.
When all the Israelites saw the fire coming down
and the glory of the LORD above the temple, they
knelt on the pavement with their faces to the
ground, and they worshiped and gave thanks to
the LORD, saying,*

"He is good;
   his love endures forever."

2 Chronicles 7:1-3

The voice of the LORD is over the waters;
   the God of glory thunders,
   the LORD thunders over the mighty waters....
The voice of the LORD twists the oaks
   and strips the forests bare.
And in his temple all cry, "Glory!"

Psalm 29:3, 9

WORSHIP

When God brings his firstborn into the world, he says,

"Let all God's angels worship him."

Hebrews 1:6

When the Magi saw the star, they were overjoyed. On coming to the house, they saw the child with his mother Mary, and they bowed down and worshiped him. Then they opened their treasures and presented him with gifts of gold and of incense and of myrrh.

Matthew 2:10-11

During the fourth watch of the night Jesus went out to them, walking on the lake.... When [he] climbed into the boat, the wind died down. Then those who were in the boat worshiped him, saying, "Truly you are the Son of God."

Matthew 14:25, 32-33

The women hurried away from the tomb, afraid yet filled with joy, and ran to tell his disciples. Suddenly Jesus met them. "Greetings," he said. They came to him, clasped his feet and worshiped him.

Matthew 28:8-9

WORSHIP

Exalt the LORD our God
  and worship at his holy mountain,
  for the LORD our God is holy.

Psalm 99:9

Shout for joy to the LORD, all the earth.
  Worship the LORD with gladness;
  come before him with joyful songs.
Know that the LORD is God.
  It is he who made us, and we are his.

Psalm 100:1-3

*Jesus said, "A time is coming and has now come
when the true worshipers will worship the Father
in spirit and truth, for they are the kind of worshipers the Father seeks. God is spirit, and his worshipers must worship in spirit and in truth."*

John 4:23-24

To him who sits on the throne and to the Lamb
be praise and honor and glory and power,
  for ever and ever!

Revelation 5:13

Devotional Thought on
WORSHIP

Solomon's magnificent temple must have been a breathtaking sight. Standing 45 feet tall and sparkling in the Jerusalem sun, its limestone walls and golden accents must have dominated the landscape of the temple mount.

The temple was a natural place to worship—a building designed by God as his royal dwelling place.

Let's talk about another magnificent building. This one is in downtown New York City. At the heart of one of the world's busiest, most populous cities is Madison Square Garden.

But can this building be a place of worship? Can Madison Square Garden—at least for a short time—take on the spiritual significance that once was reserved for Solomon's superb temple?

I think so. One night a few years ago, several Christians who play in the NBA reserved "the Garden" for a night of worship. Musical groups led the crowd in songs of praise, and at the end of the evening, evangelist Steve Jamison shared the gospel. It was a memorable night of praise, testimony and evangelism.

Wherever we are—whatever the building—we can worship God. In a hut in South America. In a rented schoolroom. In the living room of a home. We can look back in awe at Solomon's temple, but it should not make us look past the possibility of worshiping God wherever we are.

At Inspirio we love to hear from you—
your stories, your feedback,
and your product ideas.
Please send your comments to us
by way of e-mail at
icares@zondervan.com
or to the address below:

Attn: Inspirio Cares
5300 Patterson Avenue SE
Grand Rapids, MI 49530

If you would like further information
about Inspirio and the products we
create please visit us at:
www.inspiriogifts.com

Thank you and God Bless!

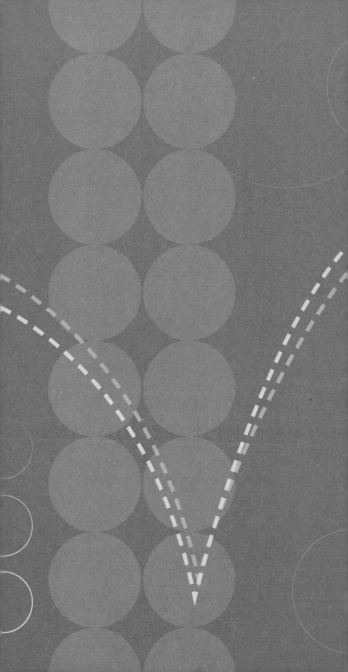